Robin R

The Pocket Essential

CONSPIRACY THEORIES

www.pocketessentials.com

First published in Great Britain 2000 by Pocket Essentials, 18 Coleswood Road, Harpenden, Herts, AL5 1EQ

Distributed in the USA by Trafalgar Square Publishing, PO Box 257, Howe Hill Road, North Pomfret, Vermont 05053

A CIP catalogue record for this book is available from the British Library.

ISBN 1-903047-30-7

9 8 7 6 5 4 3 2 1

Book typeset by Pdunk
Printed and bound by Cox & Wyman

CONTENTS

1. The World Is Not Like That

According to individual taste, the death of Princess Di was marred or enlivened by the appearance of conspiracy theories about her death. The motives of those chiefly involved in the conspiracy theorising were mixed. The main impetus behind this undoubtedly came from Dodi Al Fayed's father, Mohammed Al Fayed, and is perhaps understandable as the reaction of a grieving parent with several hundred million pounds to spend who has suddenly lost his son and his son's extremely glamorous girlfriend in a car crash. Encouraging Al Fayed's beliefs were some of the followers of Lyndon LaRouche Jnr.., a strange American conspiracy theorist whom I discuss below, who sees the evil hand of the British Royal Family behind much of the world's troubles. For LaRouche's followers it is axiomatic that the British Royals killed Di. Also contributing his 5p's worth was the former MI6 officer, Richard Tomlinson, who told the world of a British intelligence plan to kill the Serb leader Milosevic in a tunnel, using a bright light to disorientate the driver of his car. (One witness from Paris had reported seeing a flash just before Di's car crashed.)

Although the major media have lost interest in the story, there are still many Internet sites discussing her death and a recent re-examination of the evidence concluded there were still unresolved issues in the case. The "no conspiracy" verdict reached by the French legal inquiry may not be the end of the story.[1]

More recently, the death of John F Kennedy Jnr. in a plane crash was immediately surrounded by question marks which ranged from the relatively simple - people reporting phenomena during the event not reported by the mass media - to full-blown conspiracy theories about this latest dead Kennedy's alleged plans to run for president being the reason for his assassination.[2]

The stabbing of former Beatle George Harrison by a Beatles-obsessed mental patient almost immediately produced a preposterous piece of nonsense on the Net called 'Harrison Stabbing & Masonic Symbolism,' which included the following: 'Considering... the Beatles' key, pivotal role in the mass social experimentation carried out by Britain's Tavistock Institute in conjunction with covert intelligence agencies like the CIA, NSA and Britain's MI5/MI6, we'd say there is a strong likelihood that Harrison, like Lennon, was NOT the victim of some random act of senseless violence... We'd say it's a good possibility Harrison was targeted to be bumped off by some of the same forces responsible for rubbing out Lennon, using MK-Ultra/*Manchurian Candidate*-type mind-controlled assassin Mark David Chapman.'

I was more interested than I would normally have been in such twaddle because of the reference to the Tavistock Institute in London. You cannot graze in the lush fields of American conspiracy theories for long before you bump into the alleged role of the Tavistock Institute in the subversion of America in the 1960s; but I had never understood what it was the Tavistock had done to deserve this reputation. The piece about Harrison gave me a clue, telling me: 'In fact, Lennon was murdered shortly after he gave an interview to *Playboy* magazine in which he blew the lid off the fact that the Beatles were part of massive experimentation in social control/engineering unleashed by Tavistock and intelligence agencies, as was the deliberate introduction of drugs like LSD into the burgeoning 'counter-culture' scene during the 1960s and 1970s. The *Playboy* interview was published not long after Lennon's death.'

Just stop there and think about it. Had Lennon actually said any such thing it would have been a worldwide sensation; and since there was no such sensation I knew without checking that John Lennon said no such thing. Nonetheless I looked up the Lennon *Playboy* interview on the Net. I cannot pretend I read every word but, trust me, he does not mention Tavistock at all, let alone any of the rest of the nonsense attributed to him by our anonymous conspiracy theorist.[3]

The problem with the term 'conspiracy theory' is that it comes with a lot of baggage, all of it negative. Some of the baggage is recent, the accumulated warts and scars of the mountains of ridiculous piffle now littering the Internet. Some of it is historical: to most of the intellectual Western world, to politicians, academics and journalists, and to most Marxists and socialists, a conspiracy theory does not just mean a theory about a conspiracy but something much wider and negative. Conspiracy theory evokes 'the conspiracy theory of history,' the kind of mega conspiracy theory of the form: it's all the fault of, or everything is controlled by, X. In the past 300 years X has been the Jews (or Jewish bankers), the Masons, the Catholics, the Communists, the Illuminati, or the Devil. More recently we have seen mega conspiracy theories in which X is said to be the British Royal Family,[4] Aristotle Onassis,[5] the Committee of 300,[6] and the alien-US military axis.[7]

Such mega conspiracy theories strike the orthodox rational Western mind as absurd. We know that complex historical processes cannot be explained by the activities of some little group. The French and Russian revolutions, for example, cannot be explained by the existence of little cabals of Jewish bankers or Masons. The world just is not like that, is it?

Further, the term conspiracy theory has been utterly contaminated by one such mega conspiracy theory, the Jewish conspiracy theory, among whose most enthusiastic adherents was one Adolf Hitler. At worst, describing someone as 'a conspiracy theorist' evokes Hitler, the gas chambers and his insane obsession with the Jews.[8]

The result has been a virtual prohibition on the use of the term conspiracy in orthodox history or politics. For most of the chattering classes - the media and knowledge industry, academics, politicians and their assistants - to talk of conspiracy is to risk being called a conspiracy theorist; and to be described as a conspiracy theorist is the kiss of death, the intellectual equivalent of being labelled a child molester.

As a result, one of the bedrocks of the ideology of liberal democracies like ours is that conspiracy theories are always wrong, and those who believe them are mental incompetents at best. This unquestioned belief manifests itself in phrases like, 'As usual the cock-up theory of politics turned out to be true.' Belief in the cock-up theory of history and politics is at the heart of what passes for political and intellectual sophistication in liberal democracies like ours. Public genuflection before the cock-up theory of history shows that one is serious - sound, aware of the inevitable and necessary complexity of the real world; and aware, too, of the inevitable incompetence of human beings. The subtext here is: only ignorant simpletons believe the world can be explained by conspiracies.

The proponents of the classic mega conspiracy theories (Nesta Webster,[9] the John Birch Society,[10] Gary Allen,[11] Lyndon LaRouche, the various neo-fascist and neo-nazi groups still clinging to the Jewish conspiracy theory and all the others), have indeed got it wrong; but not because of their belief - let us be charitable here - that small(ish) groups of people have had an influence on history. That is an unexceptional assumption: think of Lenin and his group, or Cecil Rhodes, or the City of London, or Bill Gates. It is false information and poor or non-existent attention to basic rules of evidence and inference which discredit the classic conspiracy theory.

For example: it may be true - I have never tried to check this - that some Wall Street money ended up indirectly funding the Bolshevik revolution (a staple of the beliefs of Gary Allen, the John Birch Society and other American right-wingers). Both the British and the then smaller US money markets had invested a lot of money in Russia in the 30 years before the Bolshevik coup of 1917. It would hardly be a surprise to find all the major moneylenders of Europe, a few of whom were Jews, in there, as well. (Business was globalised then just as it is now.) When the German government funded Lenin's little group of exiled Russian revolutionaries during World War 1 in the hope that they would take Russia out of the war and thus save Germany from fighting on two fronts it is not inconceivable that some of the funds originally came from, say, loans made by non-German bankers, some of them Jewish. But many of the Americans who have found this important not only do not bother to check this factoid before recycling it, they further conclude, without evidence, that this proves that Wall Street was a bunch of Reds (or Jews, or Jewish Reds).

For example: it may be true that Masons had a part to play in both the American and French revolutions (believed by Nesta Webster). There is some evidence for both propositions.[12] But Miss Webster did not actually offer much in her books, and this tells us nothing about the power of the Masons today - or in the 1920s, for that matter, in Webster's heyday.

For example: it clearly is true that the ramified Anglo-American network, centred round the Royal Institute of International Affairs/ Chatham House in Britain and the Council on Foreign Relations in America (discussed below), has had a considerable influence in shaping British and American foreign policies, especially before World War 2. This is demonstrably true with or without Carroll Quigley's claims about the Round Table (discussed below). But this does not in any way substantiate the fantasies of the LaRouche organisation, which has incorporated Quigley into an absurd (if entertaining) tale in which

10

the UK controls America, and the British Royal Family runs the world's drug traffic, organised the assassination of John Kennedy, etc.[13]

The aversion to talk of conspiracies on the part of the intellectually respectable is thus understandable up to a point. Who wants to be associated with rubbish like LaRouche, let alone with people who think the world is being run by a cabal of American politicians and extraterrestrials? However, this legitimate and understandable allergy to mega conspiracy theories extends much further than the crazy fringe to a general prohibition on talk of conspiracy per se. Here is the American historian, Dr Jeffrey Bale, on the academic world's reactions to talk of conspiracy:

'Very few notions generate as much intellectual resistance, hostility and derision within academic circles as a belief in the historical importance or efficacy of political conspiracies. Even when this belief is expressed in a very cautious manner, limited to specific and restricted contexts, supported by reliable evidence, and hedged about with all sort of qualifications, it still manages to transcend the boundaries of acceptable discourse and violate unspoken academic taboos. The idea that particular groups of people meet together secretly or in private to plan various courses of action, and that some of these plans actually exert a significant influence on particular historical developments, is typically rejected out of hand and assumed to be the figment of a paranoid imagination. The mere mention of the word 'conspiracy' seems to set off an internal alarm bell which causes scholars to close their minds in order to avoid cognitive dissonance and possible unpleasantness, since the popular image of conspiracy both fundamentally challenges the conception most educated, sophisticated people have about how the world operates, and reminds them of the horrible persecutions that absurd and unfounded conspiracy theories have precipitated or sustained in the past. So strong is this prejudice among academics that even when clear evidence of a plot is inadvertently discovered in the course of their own research, they frequently feel compelled, either out of a sense of embarrassment or a desire to defuse anticipated criticism, to preface their account of it by ostentatiously disclaiming a belief in conspiracies. They then often attempt to downplay the significance of the plotting they have uncovered. To do otherwise, that is to make a serious effort to incorporate the documented activities of conspiratorial groups into their general political or historical analyses, would force them to stretch their mental horizons beyond customary bounds and, not infrequently, delve even further into certain sordid and politically sensitive topics. Most academic researchers clearly prefer to ignore the implications of conspiratorial politics altogether rather than deal directly with such controversial matters.' [14]

And the same processes occur within the world of politics and news gathering - as I discovered in 1986. At that time I was corresponding with Colin Wallace who was in Lewes prison. Wallace had worked for the British Army in Northern Ireland in the 1970s as an Information Officer and, later, as a psychological warfare officer. In the latter capacity he had become aware not only of various 'dirty tricks' being played in Northern Ireland, but also of the attempts by sections of the British secret state - notably MI5 - to smear the then-Labour government of Harold Wilson. To discredit him, Wallace was framed for manslaughter and sentenced to ten years.

In late 1986, just before Wallace got out of prison, my then-colleague in the magazine *Lobster*, Steve Dorril and I had been trying to get the media interested in Wallace's story. We were invited to see some people at the BBC's *Newsnight*. On informing Wallace of this, I was told that among the visitors to his psychological warfare unit, Information Policy, in Northern Ireland, had been Alan Protheroe. Twelve or thirteen years later in 1986, Alan Protheroe just happened to be Assistant Director General of the BBC. Nicknamed 'the Colonel' in the BBC, Protheroe was a part-time soldier/intelligence officer, specialising in military-media relations. That the Assistant Director General of the BBC should be a state-employed, psy-war specialist in his spare time, with all that implies about contacts with the British military-intelligence complex, seems not to have bothered BBC journalists at the time.

The point was that, unlike the journalists we had been talking to up to that point who knew nothing of Wallace's career in Northern Ireland or of the activities of Information Policy, Protheroe knew who Wallace was and what the Information Policy unit had been doing. To *News-*

night we therefore said something like this: "Protheroe is a spook; you'll have to watch him. He will probably try to prevent the broadcast of anything about Wallace." (A 'spook' is a loose description of someone who while not an officer of an intelligence or security service, is linked with or works for one.) "Really," said the BBC people we were talking to, "it isn't like that in the BBC," and dismissed what we had said.

Subsequently the *Newsnight* journalist interviewed Wallace the day he came out of prison and then had his report yanked out of a programme at the very last minute. I was watching the programme concerned and saw the confusion in the studio as the presenter tried to cope with a running order being rejigged while they were on air. We subsequently heard that Protheroe had indeed blocked the Wallace interview; but when asked, the BBC denied that they had ever interviewed Wallace. Protheroe's action was confirmed four months later in the *Sunday Times* (5 April 1987), and has been acknowledged since by a senior *Newsnight* staffer who has now left the BBC. When the Wallace story reappeared again at the end of January 1990, the BBC used some of that 'non-existent' *Newsnight* footage to illustrate various news items about him.

The response of *Newsnight* people - "it isn't like that at the BBC"- was comical, really; or preposterous. It was then only just over a year since there had been intense media interest in the revelation that the BBC actually had its own in-house MI5 office vetting BBC employees—prima facie evidence that the Corporation was exactly "like that" on occasions. The *Newsnight* people did not say "Protheroe isn't a spook," or "we'll check it out," or even "it sounds unlikely to us, but we'll bear that in mind," all of which would have been rational responses. Instead they dismissed what we had said because we were perceived to be offering them something from that most disreputable of categories, conspiracy theory.

But we had merely suggested three things:

1. Protheroe is a part-time intelligence officer.

2. In that role he knows what Wallace and Information Policy were doing.

3. Since Wallace's role and the work of Information Policy are still being denied by the British state, in our view it is probable that Protheroe will try to block transmission of Wallace's allegations.

Yet somehow these elementary and reasonable propositions triggered the Oh-dear-we-are-dealing-with-conspiracy-nutters response, which turned their brains off.

It would be difficult to exaggerate how odd this utter aversion to talk of conspiracy is - especially on the part of journalists. It can hardly be disputed that at any time there are an infinite number of political conspiracies, from the very small to the very large, going on in every industrialised society. Routine internal party politics, for example, is very largely conspiratorial, a network of interlocking cabals, plotting how to get their hands on this or that committee, group, district, meeting. Just consider the bizarre machinations which rumbled through late 1999 and into 2000 over the selection of the Labour Party candidate to stand for election as Mayor of London!

Or consider the example of the group of Labour MPs in 1980 who were planning to leave Labour and join the Social Democratic Party, then being created in secret, when it went public. In the 1980 election for leader of the Labour Party there were two candidates: Michael Foot, the candidate of the left, and Denis Healey, the candidate of the right and centre. This group of Labour MPs, who were planning to leave Labour and join the Social Democratic Party because of Labour's alleged leftwards drift, voted for left-wing candidate Michael Foot rather than Denis Healey. As one of them, Neville Sanderson, the source of this anecdote, said later, "It was important that we finished off the job. It was very important that the Labour Party as it had become was destroyed." [15]

Their votes were enough to swing the leadership Foot's way. It was also revealed by Roy Hattersley that the notorious left-wing manifesto

14

- what Gerald Kaufman MP wryly described as the longest suicide note in history - with which Labour went into the 1983 General Election, was the result of a meeting to produce a manifesto at which the right of the party proposed nothing of their own and allowed the entire left agenda through unchallenged. The right had already decided Labour would lose the 1983 election and wanted the defeat to be laid entirely at the door of the left.[16] Thus the Labour Party's drift to the left which, most political commentators agree, condemned it to the political wilderness from 1982 to 1997, was in large part the result of two conspiracies by right-wing members of the party!

At a less spectacular level, the 'pre-meeting meeting,' before the group caucus, before the formal meeting, is routine party politics, and always was. Both major political parties at the Parliamentary level are divided into factions, some open, some not. For example, in the Tory Party of the 1980s led by Margaret Thatcher, the most important faction was the 92 Group which, even after its existence had been reported in 1986, received hardly any attention by the media.[17] The 92 Group met in private and tried to influence political appointments and policies - was a political conspiracy, in short; but was never called that, of course. Paul Flynn's recent book about the Labour Party's machinations in Wales is subtitled 'A New Labour Stitch-Up' when the title would have been much more accurately 'A New Labour Conspiracy' - for a conspiracy is what it was.[18] But 'stitch-up' sounds more harmless - and does not drop one into the dreaded conspiracy camp.

Conspiracy Is Normal Politics

The point I am probably labouring is that it is only a slight exaggeration to say, as the American writer and activist of the 1960s and 70s Carl Oglesby did, that conspiracy is normal politics carried out by normal means;[19] and this is equally true of international relations and politics in which secret diplomacy and secret intelligence play major roles.[20]

Yet this banal observation would simply be rejected - and probably laughed at as ridiculous, too ridiculous to consider - by all mainstream political and intellectual circles in this country and the United States. Among the chattering classes, political sophistication demands the ritual trashing not only of the mega conspiracy theorists, who deserve it, but virtually anyone offering a conspiracy of any kind.

The respectable Anglo-American chattering classes reject all talk of conspiracy (a) because it conflicts with the model taught to them at university, and (b) because careers in British (or American) intellectual, political or media life are not aided by being identified with radical or deviant positions.

The hostility to conspiracies rests upon two false assumptions. The first is the juxtaposition of the complexity of social/political processes and the presumed simplicity of any explanation of events which has a conspiracy in it. This is false because, with the exception of small minorities who espouse mega conspiracy theories, nobody is actually suggesting that social/political events can be explained by single conspiracies. What might be called conspiracy research as opposed to conspiracy theory makes things more, not less, complex than the version served up by the respectable political classes. For example, the research into the conspiracy which killed John F Kennedy has thus far generated over 400 books, uncountable articles, half a dozen serious journals and millions of pages of declassified documents released by the US government.

The second false assumption is that there is always an either/or choice, either conspiracy or cock-up, when the real world is usually a complicated mixture of both. The Watergate affair, for example, contained a number of core conspiracies[21] - e.g. the formation of the secret White House 'plumbers' covert action group whose various illegal activities included the break-in at the Democratic Party's office. But these were overlaid with the consequences of human error (cock-up) - e.g. Nixon's White House recording system which recorded a number of incriminating conversations between Nixon and his aides. The Iran-Contra affair was triggered when a plane being used to secretly transport supplies to the Contras fighting the Nicaraguan government was shot down. One of the crew survived and, contrary to all good clandestine operational practice, he was carrying documentation which led investigators back to the White House and the hitherto secret operation - an illegal conspiracy - being run by a then-unknown Colonel, Oliver North.[22] North's operation was then further revealed when investigators found hundreds of e-mail memos to and from his office which he thought he had destroyed when he deleted them on his computer.

The denouncing of 'the conspiracy theory of history/politics,' so commonplace among our respectable higher media, academics and politicians, is usually little more than the ritual thrashing of a straw-man almost entirely of their own construction. A more rational perspective takes it for granted that there are clandestine influences - conspiracies - at work in society. Not the ridiculous, world-controlling mega conspiracies about the Masons, or the Illuminati, or Jewish bankers, or the alien 'greys,' or other such nonsense, but more mundane things like intelligence agencies manipulating domestic and international politics, or companies buying government policies by making anonymous donations to political parties, or 'lobbying.' [23]

It became absurd to deny the existence of large-scale political conspiracies, or powerful 'hidden forces,' as soon as the existence of the CIA or KGB - both vast state conspiracies - was revealed.

The irrationality of the mega conspiracy theory is rightly contrasted with the rationality of the conventional view, that things are complex. This is the concept of pluralism - the dominant political model in a liberal democracy like ours: our society's official picture of itself. Pluralism, as the term suggests, tells us that society is complex, that there are many, a plurality of, groups and interests jostling for position and power: unions; owners of capital; political parties; lobby groups; trade associations; voluntary organisations; bankers; bureaucracies, etc. This view is obviously generally true, but tells us nothing in itself; for what pluralism does not tell us is which groups of the many that exist have the power - nor how they use it. The interesting questions begin where pluralism stops.

The concept of pluralism was popularised in the 1950s and used in the post-World War 2 struggle with the Soviet Union. They had dictatorship; we had democracy. They had the secret police; we had Parliament. Conspiracy was something the Reds did. This made a degree of intellectual sense in the first 25 years of the Cold War when the existence of the Western democracies' own secret services was still more or less a secret. But it has made no sense for the last twenty years when their existence has been revealed. In Britain, for example, among the many groups in our 'pluralist' society are powerful state agencies - the armed forces, MI5, MI6, Special Branches and GCHQ, for example - whose activities are not only still largely secret, they are intrinsically conspiratorial. The British state contains and is maintained by a group

17

of official conspiracies about which the ordinary citizen is not allowed to know much; and in the case of the intelligence, security and military services, virtually nothing. To try to study the activities of organisations like the CIA or MI5 is not remotely similar to belief in mega conspiracy theories about Jewish bankers or the Illuminati. The British author Anthony Summers put it very nicely when he said he was not interested in conspiracy theories - i.e. the mega variety - but he was interested in theories about conspiracies.

Here is one of the American conspiracy world's leading figures, the highly entertaining Robert Anton Wilson. Wilson was co-author of the fictional *Illuminatus Trilogy*, [24] the first volume of which contained a very acute and funny parody of American mega conspiracy theorists of the 1960s and 70s:

'As Edward Luttwak documents in his cheerfully Machiavellian little text, *The Coup d'Etat*, more governments have been changed since World War 2 by the coup d'état than by any other method. More governments have been changed by coup than by all the democratic elections and revolutions combined. Since every coup is by definition a conspiracy, this means that conspiracies have had more effect on the past 40 years of world history than all the electoral politics and all the popular revolutions added together. That is rather ominous, in a period when 'educated' opinion holds that it is infamous, nutty, eccentric or downright paranoid to think about conspiracies at all. We are, in effect, forbidden to think about how the planet is actually governed.' [25]

Wilson is obviously exaggerating for rhetorical effect but his general point is well taken. The mysterious thing is not that some poor deluded fools insist on seeing conspiracies, but how it is that, for so long, so many apparently intelligent people - most Anglo-American political scientists and journalists, for example - have managed not to notice that conspiracy is an everyday and rather important part of the phenomena they purport to be studying and reporting. Let me give some more examples.

Since its formation in the 1920s until its demise about 10 years ago, an organisation called the Economic League collected and spent, in today's money, millions of pounds every year working against the British left. It produced propaganda - leaflets, planted newspaper articles, employed full-time speakers, ran courses - and maintained a blacklist of 'subversives,' access to which was given to employers who paid an annual subscription. It may have spent as much money as the Conser vative Party since World War 1. Yet there was not one academic essay on and virtually no journalistic investigation of the Economic League between its formation and 1988.[26] No history of British domestic politics in the twentieth century can be anything but incomplete without the Economic League, but I have never seen one that contains such an account.[27]

Orthodox American contemporary history and politics somehow manage to skip over the fact that in a five-year period in the 60s, one president, the probable next president, and the most important black leader since the war were victims of assassinations which were never investigated properly and remain unsolved.

One Of Those No-Weatherman-Required Situations

Britain has been run for most of this century by two intensely secretive, overlapping groups: one is the British state, about which we know very little, thanks to this country's secretive culture. This is especially true of its secret branches about which even MPs are not allowed to ask questions. The other is the Conservative Party - even its members know almost nothing about who has funded it in the last 100 years.[28] In the USA since World War 2, in the name of National Security and justified by the Cold War with the Soviet Union, a group of government military and intelligence agencies, headed by the CIA and the Pentagon, with their satellite supply companies - the military industrial complex in short - have been operating largely in secret; and very profitably, too. It is hard sometimes to show the links between the dominant political ideas and the interests of a society, but in these instances it looks pretty straightforward: the most powerful interests in Britain and the United States do not want their secret activities examined and - surprise! what a coincidence! - it turns out that being interested in secret activities - in conspiracies - is intellectually disreputable in both societies.

Notes

1. A recent survey of the case reported the existence of over 30,000 websites referring to the subject. See Terry Hanstock, 'Di's Death Re-examined' in *Lobster* 38, December 1999 (www.lobster-magazine.co.uk). Try the newsgroup at alt.conspiracy.princess-diana. One of those engaged in these on-going discussions recommended the following as the best Diana conspiracy sites:

> www.anaserve.com/~wethepeople/diforum
> www.dianaconspiracy.homepage.com/
> www.elint.server101.com/affairofstate.htm.

2. See the website of conspiracy theorist Anthony J Hilder, which had posted 20 stories on this subject a couple of weeks after the incident. www.freeworldalliance.com.

3. Which still does not answer the question: what is the origin of the idea that the Tavistock Institute in London played some sinister role in the 1960s?

4. The views of the organisation headed by Lyndon LaRouche Jnr.. These are perhaps best expressed in the book by two of his followers, *Dope Inc!* There is a reasonable chapter on LaRouche in Jonathan Vanakin's *Conspiracies Cover-ups And Crimes* (New York: Dell, 1992). The occasional LaRouchie I have encountered came across a bit like paranoid, politicised - not unintelligent - evangelical Christians. The conversation proceeds fairly rationally up to a certain point at which you can feel the steel shutters in their brains coming down. The LaRouche organisation is at www.larouchepub.com.

5. The so-called Skeleton Key to the Gemstone File, a conspiracy theory in which the author, the late Bruce Roberts, attributes to Aristotle Onassis, among other things, the assassination of John and Robert Kennedy and the real cause of the Watergate scandal. This has been the subject of two full-length studies and a more recent collection of essays edited by Kenn Thomas and David Hatcher Childress, *Inside The Gemstone File* (Kempton, Illinois, USA: Adventures Unlimited Press, 1999). This writer published the first critique of The Gemstone File, published in *The International Times* in 1978. This is included in the Thomas/Childress book. The Gemstone File is a strange mixture of facts and fantasies, most of the key allegations being uncheckable; most that are checkable being false. Despite this it has now been circu-

lating for over 25 years. The American writer Martin Cannon possesses the original letters by Bruce Roberts from which the Skeleton Key was extracted. He e-mailed me extracts in early 2000 and they show that Bruce Roberts was a nutcase.

6. British author John Coleman publishes a newsletter, *World In Review*, and believes the Committee of 300 is running the world. Now resident in the USA, Coleman claims to be a former member of the British secret service. Of his background I know nothing. Of his claims to have been a member of the Secret Intelligence Service I am profoundly sceptical; but since the SIS does not publish a list of employees, past and present, I can say no more.

7. I am unaware of any reputable books on this specific theme but it is believed among certain sections of the American UFO buff world and is centred around the documents purporting to reveal the existence of a stratum of US government officials with access to the information about aliens and certain advanced technologies which they are alleged to have either given to us earthlings, or which earthlings have devised for themselves, 'reverse engineering' them from crashed UFOs. Try www.ufomind.com/ufo/topic/mj12. The so-called MJ12 documents on which this is based have been much discussed. One of those who believes them to be genuine is Stanton Friedman. See his *Top Secret / Majic* (London: Michael O'Mara, 1997). This writer is sure they are a fabrication, part of a fairly sophisticated disinformation programme run by elements within the US military. But I would have trouble proving it; and Friedman makes a surprisingly strong case in defence of their authenticity. The disinformation aspect is discussed below.

8. On which, most recently, see *The History Of An Obsession: German Judeophobia And The Holocaust*, Klaus P Fischer (London: Constable, 1998). This conflation of conspiracy theory with the Holocaust was illustrated recently when the *Washington Post* of 12 December 1999, commenting on the civil trial which concluded that James Earl Ray had not killed Dr Martin Luther King, wrote: 'The deceit of history, whether it occurs in the context of Holocaust denial or in an effort to rewrite the story of Dr King's death, is a dangerous impulse for which those committed to reasoned debate and truth cannot sit still.' (Incidentally, given the role of the *Post* in not investigating - for example - the murder of Dr King, the idea that it is committed to 'reasoned debate and truth' is hilarious.)

9. English author of the 1920s and 30s, discussed below.

10. On which see, for example, 'The John Birch Society,' Allan Westin in *The Radical Right*, ed. Daniel Bell (New York: Doubleday, Anchor, 1964).

11. Co-author of one of the most influential of the John Birch books, *None Dare Call It Conspiracy*, (Seal Beach, California: Concord Press, many editions in the 70s). His co-author Larry Abraham wrote a much less well-known sequel, *Call It Conspiracy* (Seattle: Double A Publications, 1985).

12. See J M Roberts, *The Mythology Of The Secret Societies* (St Albans: Paladin, 1972).

13. I first came across the LaRouche organisation in Bonn, Germany, in 1979. They had a stall on the pavement selling LaRouche's books and magazines. The one that caught my eye, which I bought, had above the masthead the slogan, 'End British Control Of America.' You what? thought I, and reached for my Deutschmarks. More than twenty years after the group's first appearance, no one is sure what the group is doing or who - if anyone - is funding it.

14. Jeffrey M Bale, ' "Conspiracy Theories" And Clandestine Politics' in *Lobster* 29. The historian Thomas Mahl did his PhD on the British covert operations in the US between 1939 and the US entry into World War 2. A fascinating thesis, but very badly written. In 1998 his thesis was published as a book. Here is his reaction to an accusation that his work is conspiratorial: 'How does the historian avoid the charge that he is indulging in conspiracy history when he explores the activities of a thousand people, occupying two floors of Rockefeller Center, in their efforts to involve the United States in a major war?' From a review by Justin Raimondo of *Desperate Deception: British Covert Operations In The United States, 1939-1944* by Thomas F Mahl, as published in the December 1998 *Chronicles* issue (pp.24-6) and reproduced on *A-Albionic Research Weekly Update* of 3 April 2000. http://a albionic.com/a-albionic.html.

15. *The Sunday Telegraph*, 14 January 1996.

16. Hattersley's comments in 'Comrades At War,' part of the series *The Witness Years*, BBC2, December 1995.

17. See 'Lost Legions Of The Right' by Julian Critchley MP, *The Observer*, 10 August 1986. Even Critchley, a Tory MP, is unsure of the 92 Group's origins, writing that it 'was raised some years ago...'

18. Paul Flynn MP, *Dragons Led By Poodles: The Inside Story Of A New Labour Stitch-Up* (London: Politicos Publishing, 1999).

19. Oglesby is the author of one of the best books about US conspiratorial politics, *The Yankee And Cowboy War: Conspiracies From Dallas To Watergate And Beyond* (New York: Berkeley Medallion Books, 1977).

20. A good illustration of this thesis is the recent history of Cyprus, Brendan O'Malley and Ian Craig's *The Cyprus Conspiracy* (London: I B Tauris, 1999) which describes a long succession of conspiracies by the US and UK governments in the post-World War 2 era to divide the Greek Cypriots from the Turkish Cypriots and so retain US and UK military bases on the island.

21. The recent book on post-World War 2 Cyprus, referred to in footnote 20 above, contains evidence of many interlocking, competing, overlapping conspiracies.

22. This is described in detail by one of the journalists who followed the story from this beginning, Robert Parry. See his *Lost History: Contras, Cocaine, The Press And 'Project Truth'* (Arlington, Virginia: The Media Consortium, 1999).

23. The day I was writing this paragraph *The Independent* carried yet another report on the affair of former German Chancellor Kohl and the secret funds he received from business sources and the French state.

24. It says something about the wacky world of conspiracy theorists that some people ignored the fact that the book was fiction and claimed that Wilson and his co-author were telling the truth... disguised as fiction, of course.

25. From 'The Spaghetti Theory Of Conspiracy,' Robert Anton Wilson's introduction to Donald Holmes, *Illuminati Conspiracy - The Sapien System*, (© 1987, New Falcon Publications, 655 East Thunderbird, Phoenix, AZ 85022, USA) posted on the Internet sometime in 1999.

26. The first academic writing on the League was Arthur McIvor, "A Crusade For Capitalism': The Economic League, 1919-39' in *The Journal Of Contemporary History*, Vol. 23, 1988. My comments about the academic historians applies equally to the British left. How could they expect to defeat an enemy about whom they knew so little?

27. As I wrote that last paragraph my eye was caught by one of the standard popular post-World War 2 political histories of Britain, Alan Sked and Chris Cook's, *Post-War Britain: A Political History*, on the shelf above my desk. Its index has no references to intelligence services, security services, MI5, MI6, IRD, the Economic League, Aims of Industry or the CIA. Their omission is partly because in such a short, general work covering a large subject, these areas do not make the final edit; but also because these subjects are still not regarded as proper objects of academic study.

28. The funding of the Conservative Party is another of those subjects which academic political scientists have managed not to study in the twentieth century. The first book on the subject was by a non-academic, Colin Challen. See his *Price Of Power: The Secret Funding Of The Tory Party* (London: Vision, 1998).

2. I Am Paranoid But Am I Paranoid Enough?

To the dismay of the intellectually orthodox, we are living through a veritable golden age - or nightmare - of conspiracy theories. Compare and contrast this situation with, say, 1963. Who was interested in conspiracy theories in 1963? In the UK, there was a handful of disgruntled racist Tories - the League of Empire Loyalists who became one of the foundation blocks of the National Front - and little groups of Hitler lovers clinging to the old Jewish-banking-world-domination myth.[1] In the US, there was the John Birch Society, some other fringe far-right groups and a handful of Jew-haters and American Hitler freaks.[2] Conspiracy theories were out on the margin of the margins in 1963. These days we have got conspiracy theories everywhere, about almost everything; and belief in the existence of conspiracies has now penetrated large areas of popular American - and thus by import - British popular culture.

For example, in the 1990s movie *The Rock*, Sean Connery played a British SAS officer who stole former FBI chief J Edgar Hoover's secret files in the 1960s and who has been illegally imprisoned ever since.[3] The final scene of the film shows the Connery character's sidekick, played by Nicholas Cage, picking up the files, hidden by Connery years before. As he and his girlfriend drive off, Cage's character holds up a strip of microfilm and says to her, "Want to know who really killed Kennedy?"

For example, the film *Conspiracy Theory* starred Mel Gibson playing the victim of a US government mind-control programme. For the first half of the film Gibson's character is portrayed as the demented, paranoid, conspiracy theorist so loved by orthodox academia and the media; in the second half his paranoia is shown to have a rational base.

Most significant of all has been the popularity of the TV programme *The X-Files* whose thematic material is a virtual compendium of American conspiracy theories of the last two decades. With *The X-Files*, what had previously been in the background - or underground - suddenly appeared in the foreground. On the back of *The X-Files*, a large media bubble was built in this country, at the height of which there were five professionally produced, full-colour, nationally distributed magazines (and one multi-part work) devoted to the so-called *X-Files* agenda - i.e. to conspiracy theories and the paranormal.

If conspiracy theories have been in the mainstream for a while, in early 2000 conspiracy theorists began getting onto mainstream television. Britain's Channel Four, for example, broadcast half a dozen programmes made by the website disinfo.com which carries a lot of conspiracy theories. *Steamshovel*'s Kenn Thomas appeared on the Canadian Broadcasting Corporation's *Undercurrents* programme on 20 February, and *The Konformist*'s Robert Sterling regularly reported in 1999 the interest of this or that branch of the major media in his website.[4]

There are conspiracy theories in other countries. Depressingly, anti-Semitic theories are all over place: in the former Soviet Union and its former empire since the fall of the Berlin Wall in 1989 (there were distinct Jewish conspiracy theory tinges to Solidarity in Poland in the 1980s); on the right of Japanese politics even though there are no Jews in Japan. In France, Le Pen's National Front contains reminders of the French pre-World War 2 Jew-haters; and the notorious Czarist forgery from the turn of the century *The Protocols Of The Learned Elders Of Zion* is still being distributed in the Arab world as if it was a real document which could explain the existence of Israel in its midst.[5] No doubt if I knew more languages I would find conspiracy theories in all industrialised societies. But in the UK we are getting American conspiracy theories along with our American soap operas and fast-food chains. The major exception to this is the Australian-based magazine *Nexus* which carries *The X-Files* agenda of the paranormal and conspiracy theories plus other examples of 'suppressed' or alternative knowledge in the fields of science, energy and health. When I first saw *Nexus* I assumed it was American (and indeed, much of its contents is).[6]

Most American conspiracy theories come from white people. There are some conspiracy theories in the Afro-American community. Some of the black American religious subcultures believed that Reagan had 666, the biblical mark of the beast, tattooed on the back of his skull, under his hair; others have believed that the distribution of heroin among the black population was a plot by the government to keep black Americans down. Currently a substantial section of African Americans believe that the CIA was selling crack cocaine to help finance the war against Nicaragua after Congress cut off the funds for the war. A similar sort of theory is the idea that AIDS was a biological warfare experiment which escaped. A variation on this is the idea enthusiastically propagated by the KGB's disinformation people, that AIDS was a germ warfare experiment designed by whites to kill blacks. Joshua Nkomo in Zimbabwe was expounding this thesis a couple of years ago - his son died of AIDS. In 1990 a survey was reported in *The New York Times* (29 October) which showed that 30% of Afro-Americans in New York City believed AIDS was an ethno-specific virus designed by the US military.[7] But American conspiracy theories - at any rate the ones which get reported or get attention on the Net - seem to be primarily a white phenomenon; and primarily a white male phenomenon (though there are a few prominent women).[8]

Most people could produce a list of wacky conspiracy theories with very little research. Here are a few examples I came across, without looking for them, in a couple of months a few years ago. A number of books about the O J Simpson case appeared in the US after the trial. According to a contents summary I read in the catalogue of Tom Davis Books,[9] one such argues that the murders had their origins in the FBI blacklist of certain bar applicants - i.e. would-be lawyers - because of their anti-war activities. Unemployed for years, these unemployed lawyers assassinated Nicole Simpson and framed O J Simpson to compel the FBI to disclose the blacklist. Only in America, with one million lawyers, the home of the lawyer joke, would someone imagine a murderous cabal of unemployed lawyers!

For a mere £95, somebody called Michael Todd, in Yorkshire, offered to provide evidence of a conspiracy called Operation PELT, with a secret HQ in Ireland and 30 offices worldwide. The aim of PELT, he claimed, is to destroy the entire alternative movement; health, green, eco, etc. I wrote asking for a sample of his evidence but did not get a reply.

The administrator of the anti-fluoride National Pure Water Association, wrote to me suggesting that the reason for the vilification of Yorkshire Water during the drought of 1995, was not Yorkshire Water's inability of provide water to all their customers while paying their directors and shareholders large salaries and dividends, but their refusal to add fluoride to their water. She wrote: 'Much of the persecution of that company this year - leaks, dry reservoirs, etc. - is, we are

27

sure, orchestrated *punishment* for their decision.' (Emphasis added.) I wrote asking her for evidence, but received no reply.[10]

A UFO buff I know slightly tried to persuade me that the US have a secret base built under Loch Lomond in Scotland, from which emerge mysterious craft. (The UFO as underwater craft is one of the minor themes amongst UFO theories.) Why, said I, would they put such a base under the single most popular tourist spot on the west of Scotland, visited every day by hundreds, if not thousands of people?

The difficulty - or the delight - is the fact that buried in the stupid nonsense there is often something of interest in almost all of these, and similar, subjects. A conspiracy of disgruntled unemployed lawyers seems an unlikely explanation of the O J Simpson case but - who knows? - improbable though it sounds now, one day someone may show that O J was framed (which is the conspiracy theory believed by the majority of black Americans).

The anti-fluoride case, after years of being high on the crank list, is creeping into the mainstream. There are still water companies in the UK which are unable or unwilling to put fluoride in their water supplies because of local opposition. Even *Covert Action*, the very serious, American, spy-watching journal, has published an article on the fluoride issue, Joel Griffiths' 'Fluoride: Commie Plot Or Capitalist Ploy?' - something that would have been unimaginable a few years before when the fluoride issue was discussed almost exclusively by the far right.[11] The 'Commie plot' in the title of Griffiths' paper refers to the belief in some sections of the US far right of the 1950s and 60s that fluoridation was a Communist conspiracy to pollute America's water. This was ridiculed in the Stanley Kubrick film *Dr Strangelove* by the portrait of the crazed US base commander, Jack D Ripper (sic), played by the late great Sterling Hayden, which probably put the anti-fluoride case back a generation in the process.

Good conspiracy theories never die: this is one of their defining features. No matter how stupid they are and how frequently they are refuted, they cannot be got rid of; there is always another cohort of believers coming through to replace those who have abandoned the theory. On 29 June 1999, the Rumour Mills News Agency, carried on *The Konformist* Internet newswire, referred to a paper that was allegedly introduced in a Congressional hearing by a Russian defector. (It's getting flaky already...) This paper, purporting to be a Soviet report on the fluoridation of the American water supply, allegedly said that fluoride was known to cause neurological changes in the brains of children which reduces their IQ. The paper supported a planned attack on America by fluoridating their water supply, reducing the intelligence level of Americans, and making a take-over of future generations of Americans much easier. So it was a Commie plot after all![12] In fact, as Joel Griffiths' paper shows, the origins of the dumping of fluoride in drinking water lay in the desire of the US companies, who produced the otherwise useless and toxic fluoride as a by-product of other processes, to find a means of disposing of it. Dumping it in reservoirs was a terrific solution for them! There is a real case to answer from the anti-fluoride lobby, though it has yet to be taken seriously by the major media in this country or - oddly enough - by the growing consumer lobby concerned with the quality of the food we eat.

There surely is not a US base under Loch Lomond; and there surely is not a secret conspiracy between the alien 'greys' and the US government; and there surely are not tens of thousands of Americans being kidnapped and sexually assaulted by aliens. But - and this is a big 'but' - this does not mean that the entire UFO thing can be rationally written off as nonsense, hallucinations, weather balloons, experimental US aircraft or whatever. There are now too many videotapes of strange things in the sky to support the many reports from sensible, rational people: the ubiquitous camcorder may yet resolve lots of this for us. And how do we explain the fact that thousands of Americans - it is mostly Americans as yet - experience and report being abducted by aliens? Whitley Strieber, author of *Communion*, describing his own encounters with aliens, reported in one of its sequels *Confirmation*, that he received 30,000 (!) letters from people describing similar experiences among a total mailbag of 250,000. Since British Members of Parliament sit up and take notice if they get a couple of dozen letters on a subject, to get 30,000 letters on anything is absolutely astonishing - as is the fact that at least 30,000 people apparently have memories of something like, or reminiscent of, abduction by aliens. The alien abduction phenomenon is bizarre in the extreme and no one - certainly no one on the sceptical side of the argument - has come within shooting distance of providing an explanation of what is going on.

Behind a surprising number of the bizarre stories floating around in the cosmic conspiracy miasma there is something - maybe just a fragment - which is real. Sometimes even the most implausible claim has to be taken seriously. For over twenty years a handful of people have claimed that the US never went to the moon. It was all faked in a movie studio, they said, a large-scale piece of political propaganda in the Cold War with the Soviet Union. The 1978 film *Capricorn One*, with one O J Simpson among its cast, dealt with this in fictional form - an early example of the post-Watergate conspiracy climate being reflected in Hollywood. At first glance this is just profoundly implausible - stupid, really. A conspiracy that big would involve hundreds, maybe thousands of people keeping quiet for decades. It just could not be done, could it? Even if you can envisage the American government's national security bureaucracy approving such a high-risk plan - and I cannot - it would be impossible to keep it secret. Somebody would talk; something would leak; somebody would sell the story to the media for big bucks.[13]

But - even here there is a 'but' - a photographic expert is now claiming that some of the photographs given out by NASA as shots of the moon landings were done in a studio. There was a long, careful, and I think totally convincing, analysis published in the *Fortean Times* in January 1997. But even if true, what does this suggest? Do fake pictures mean a fake moon-landing? As a federally-funded bureaucracy, NASA's aim was to achieve maximum publicity to enable it to screw maximum dollars out of Congress for future projects. It is more likely, surely, that NASA just dummied up some photographs on earth; you get better pictures in a studio than on the moon. In a studio, for example, you can spotlight the US flag on the otherwise rather dimly-lit lunar module... And so 25 years later, a photographer looking at these photographs thinks, 'hang on a minute... on the moon there is only one source of light - so where has the spotlight in this photograph come from?'

Over a decade ago I met someone who believed that derogatory information about him was being inserted into novels and radio programmes. He pointed out paragraphs which he thought seemed to be aimed at him. The evidence was not convincing: there was nothing in the paragraphs that he pointed out to me. 'How is the material fed out to the writers?' I asked. 'That's obvious,' he replied, 'through the publishers' secret society.' But of this society there was not a shred of evidence, I pointed out. In any case, he was manifesting all kinds of other symptoms of paranoia: all his phone calls were taped, he thought his house was bugged, etc. It was text-book paranoia, I concluded my visit by telling him that I thought he was crazy and should see a psychiatrist. Some months later he sent me a photocopy of an article containing the first exposé of the British publishers' secret society, precisely as he had hypothesised.[14] I replied that this was definitely one for him but I still did not believe his story. The fact that a secret society had been discovered inside the British publishing world did not make up for the fact that there was nothing in the books or in the radio programmes he indicated that could reasonably be interpreted the way he was doing.

Paranoia And The Paranormal

Why there is a link between an interest in the paranormal, the occult, strange phenomena and an interest in conspiracy theories is unclear to me but it is real. This connection is reflected in my own life. I was casually interested in the paranormal from the late 1960s after finding a book in the public library about radionics - the 'black box,' object of much ridicule in those days - and came across US conspiracy theories six years later. Even so I am unsure of the meaning of the link. The best I could come up with would be as banal as this: perhaps if you are willing to believe that the orthodoxy is wrong in one area - say, the reality or non-reality of the paranormal - you are likely to consider that other orthodoxies could be wrong. It may simply be down to personality types. However it is explained, interest in the two areas seems to have developed in parallel.[15]

In the UK, the landmarks on what might loosely be called the paranormal side of the agenda seem to me to have been the following.

First, the book by Pauwels and Bergier, *The Dawn Of Magic* (or *The Morning Of The Magicians*, its American title), first published in the UK in 1963. It was Pauwels and Bergier who brought to a mass audience in Britain the subjects of psychic powers, apparent links between the occult and the Nazi regime in Germany, UFOs, strange anomalies in the natural world, theories about the pyramids and so forth.

Second was the series of books by the English writer John Michell, most famously *The Flying Saucer Vision* in 1967. This introduced ley lines, geomancy, numerology, and extraterrestrials - the whole earth mysteries thing.[16]

The third landmark was the book *Psychic Discoveries Behind The Iron Curtain* by two *Reader's Digest* journalists in 1970 which showed that the Soviet Union's government was funding research into psychic and paranormal phenomena. This was enormously significant because if a strictly materialist and anti-religious culture like the Soviet Union was taking the subject seriously, it was hard to argue, as most of science then did in the West, that this was all mystical nonsense.

Fourth was the emergence of Uri Geller and Matthew Manning in the mid-1970s - especially Geller, who appeared to demonstrate powers beyond the known laws of physics - and was doing it on television.[17]

The fifth significant feature was people like Erich von Danniken who popularised much of this material with tales of strange phenomena - the Bermuda Triangle, pyramids, Space Gods and so forth.

Sixth, throughout this period, in the background then, was the UFO mystery which culminated in Spielberg's films *Close Encounters Of The Third Kind* and *ET. Close Encounters* was a brilliant synthesis of the then (1977)-dominant versions of the UFO contact story, as well as incorporating threads from other areas - for example, the flight of US aeroplanes which apparently disappeared in the Bermuda Triangle.

And seventh, the current explosion of UFO reports, stories of abductions, contacts, and landings by extraterrestrials which we are getting via the United States.[18]

This torrent of information, of alternative this, that and everything,[19] has resulted in extraordinary artefacts such as the *Frontiers Science* catalogue, which offers books or videotapes on Lost Civilisations - MU, Atlantis, Lemuria - and a host of others in Africa, Central and South America.[20] It has cryptozoology - Big Foot, Sasquatch, Yeti; giants, sea monsters; crop circles; Stonehenge and all the other stone architecture before Christ; extraterrestrial archaeology allegedly showing buildings on Mars and the Moon; anti-gravity devices; UFOs and aliens; free energy devices; Tesla technology; alternative science and treatments of every kind from cold fusion to radionics and Wilhelm Reich's orgone boxes; ley lines, earth mysteries; geomancy - and a section called conspiracy and history.[21] It is this body of knowledge - let us call it 'knowledge' - which has provided the thematic background to *The X-Files* and *Dark Skies* on TV and dozens of films coming across the Atlantic.

The merging of the paranormal and the parapolitical in *The X Files* and its derivatives has been good and bad news for those of us trying to deal rationally with political conspiracy theories. The good news has been the massive exposure of certain parapolitical themes - e.g. the conspiratorial activities of US state organisations and the influence of elites on a supposed democracy - to a mass TV audience. But this has been massively outweighed by the association of those themes with junk UFO conspiracy theories.

Notes

1. See, for example, George Thayer, *The British Political Fringe* (London: Anthony Blond, 1965).

2. See George Thayer, *The Farther Shore Of Politics* (London: Allan Lane/Penguin, 1968).

3. Hoover's secret files were also the subject matter of the best Robert Ludlum novel, *The Chancellor Manuscript* (1977).

4. Website www.tv.cbc.ca/undercurrents

5. *The Independent*, 4 February 2000 reported that the Defence Ministry of the Syrian government 'runs its own publishing house that has printed an Arabic edition of that hoary old forgery, *The Protocols Of The Elders Of Zion*.'

6. Its UK edition is said to be selling 20,000 copies. *Nexus* has a website at www.peg.apc.org/~nexus/

7. There is a surprising (to me) amount of evidence to support this view - or what looks like evidence. I am not equipped scientifically to evaluate this and thus far the orthodox scientific community seems to have ignored it. Go to www.tetrahedron.org and look at the information on the book by Dr Horowitz. Or go to www.konformist.com/1999/aids/aids.htm or www.konformist.com/1999/aids/manmade.txt

8. I am not sure how this connects but there is a link here to the attitude of some feminists in the 1980s who saw investigative journalism - also heavily dominated by men - as 'stupid macho boys' games.'

9. One of the pioneers of mail-order conspiracy books at www.tdbooks.com

10. National Pure Water Association, 12 Dennington Lane, Crigglestone, Wakefield, WF4 3ET.

11. In *Covert Action Information Bulletin* 42 (Fall 1992). See also Joel Griffiths and Chris Bryson, 'Fluoride, Teeth And The Atomic Bomb' in *Watershed* (Journal of the National Pure Water Association), vol. 3 no. 3.

12. www.rumormillnews.com, 29 June 1999. The column included this fairly typical piece of conspiracy theorist thinking: 'In the last week, I have read two websites that cover the physical illnesses that are caused by two different chemicals: Aspartame and Fluoride. *It is obvious to me* that the big chemical and pharmaceutical companies are engaging in a wholesale poisoning of the world to enhance their profits. (They may also be doing this to 'dumb down' the people of the world so they can be easily subdued when the One World Totalitarian government kicks in.)' (Emphasis added.)

13. The sharp-eyed reader may have spotted that this is precisely the line argued by the CIA against the Warren Commission critics in 1967! In my defence let me comment that the Kennedy assassination could have been done by a handful of people: faking a moon shot could not.

14. Christopher Hurst, 'A Touch Of The Leather Aprons' in *The Bookseller*, 19 August 1988.

15. For example, I was twice invited to speak on conspiracy theories at the annual conference of the *Fortean Times*, the UK's leading journal of strange phenomena. Apparently for the Forteans, conspiracy theories are another example of strange phenomena...

16. How far we've come since then is suggested by the appearance on Sunday, 23 March 1996 of an article in the *Sunday Telegraph* travel and tourism section on ley lines in England; or the wide acceptance of feng shui, a domestic adaptation of geomancy, these days. In 1966 there was not one book in print in the UK about ley lines and no one had heard of feng shui.

17. On Geller see the very interesting biography, Jonathan Margolis, *Uri Geller: Magician Or Mystic?* (London: Orion, 1998). Margolis began the book convinced that Geller was a fraud and ended up a believer. It is widely believed among the British media that in some way Geller has been exposed as a fraud by the Amazing Randi. As Margolis discovered, to his surprise, this is not so. There are obvious parallels with the story of Doug and Dave who claimed to have made some 'fake' crop circles. The fact that Doug and Dave could not possibly have made all the UK circles, let alone the circles appearing all over the world, meant nothing to the British mass media which chuckled, printed 'idiot circle believers hoaxed' stories, and consigned the subject to the dustbin. Meanwhile, without the assistance of Doug and Dave, crop circles go on appearing in the UK... Matthew Manning these days seems to work solely as a healer but the book about his early life, *The Link* (New York: Holt, Rinehart and Winston, 1975) is worth getting from the library.

18. In the last few years it has been revealed that American as well as Soviet military and intelligence services have been examining many of these areas since the late 1960s - while routinely rubbishing other people who pursued them. See for example Jim Schnabel, *Remote Viewers: The Secret History Of America's Psychic Spies* (New York: Dell, 1997) and Armen Victorian, *Mind Controllers* (London: Vision, 1998), chapters 9 and 10.

19. An acquaintance of mine reported that, in late 1999, in a London branch of Waterstone's bookshop, the section headed 'Alternative History' was considerably bigger than the section just marked 'History.'

20. Without apparent anxiety it offers five conflicting identifications and locations for Atlantis, including one claiming that Atlantis was the state of Wisconsin in the USA! Website www.f-s-f-com

21. This catalogue - and others like it - is striking in what it does not offer to its readers. Its 'Conspiracy And History' section includes not one book by any of the serious American researchers of conspiracies, nor any of the many serious, well-researched and documented books on the Kennedy assassination. In these areas it offers some of the fringe writers - in effect the alternative writers to the established alternative.

3. From Blue Skies To Dark Skies

America - and to a lesser extent Britain - has been awash in conspiracy theories and the paranormal for the past decade, maybe more. In the late 1990s some people attributed this to PMT - Pre-Millennial Tension. It is clear that this was not a very significant factor - the millennium celebrations have gone and the conspiracy theories are still with us - though it added a peculiarly millennial flavour to some of the conspiracy theorists on the American Christian fringe.[1] The proliferation of conspiracy theories is attributable to more prosaic factors: the failing US empire, recent developments in reprographic and communication technologies, and the actual events in US political history since the 60s.

Although the triumphalist post-Cold War rhetoric may mask this, the American Dream is faltering. At best, real wage rates are no higher than they were twenty years ago for many of the working class in America. For some they are lower. The days when a middle-class American family could afford to put their children through college on one (generally male) salary are over. There are thousands of homeless people on the streets of all the big American cities. The gap between the top income stratum in the US and the bottom is wider than it has been since the war, and getting wider every year. America now has 25% of the world's prisoner population (cf. 3% of the world's population) - most of them black, most of them there for possession of drugs - in its booming prison system.[2] The talk on the American left of an American prison gulag is not entirely specious. Things are not going according to plan for many of the white middle- and working-class Americans and they need to explain this to themselves.

Surveys regularly report that only around 2% of adult Americans read books of any kind. Most American newspapers and magazines barely mention the outside world, and the primary source of information for most Americans is television. But most American television simply does not deal with real political and economic issues in enough depth for the average American citizen to understand something as complicated as the economic decline of a great power. Faced with 30, 60, 120 cable TV channels putting out varieties of piffle at best, and with tabloid comics like the *National Inquirer* (the forerunner of the

British *Daily Sport*) and all its imitators in supermarkets putting out honest-to-God inventions as 'news,' it is little wonder that Mrs and Mrs Joe Six-pack have trouble understanding the world and distinguishing between what is real and what is a fake.[3] And the Six-packs may have been 'born again.' By the standards of secular Britain, America is a profoundly religious society. People who believe in God and the Devil, who think *The Bible* is the literal account of the creation of the world,[4] do not have that far to go to believe that the sky at night is swarming with UFOs looking for people to abduct and experiment on; or that the United States government is about to surrender control of the US to the United Nations in the name of the New World Order; or that Bill Clinton's administration has prepared concentration camps ready to incarcerate 'the patriots' who might resist these changes.[5]

You can see the change of mood reflected in the US accounts of encounters with extraterrestrials. In the 1950s, when the US empire was booming, and the average white American consumer was experiencing continuously increasing material prosperity, the extraterrestrials reportedly meeting the American citizen, were largely benign,[6] making contact with the world with advice and friendship. Now that the US economic empire is no longer delivering ever-increasing wealth for the vast majority of its white citizens, and sections of the big American cities are turning into facsimiles of the set of the film *Blade Runner*, the skies over America at night are apparently bustling with alien rapists, beaming down into peoples' bedrooms to scoop them up and take them away for extended sessions of sexual abuse, implantation of mind-control devices and experiments.

In the 1950s white America had blue skies.

Today it has *Dark Skies*.

Many Americans perceive things going wrong - but not why. Not only are the information and the concepts they need not readily available, Americans are handicapped in their ability to understand the world by the power of the American myth. America is the country of Manifest Destiny, bearing the shining torch of freedom and democracy, the land of the brave and the home of the free. Most important and most inhibiting, America is a country whose official myth is that anyone can make it and become rich if they try hard enough. So deeply

Explanation?

ingrained is this myth, many Americans simply find it impossible to believe that there is something wrong with their economic and social system. But if the system is fine, and things are going wrong what is causing the problem? The answer is, of course, that things are going wrong because of the actions of... bad people: and they are doing it behind everybody's backs. This must be the case because most people cannot see them doing it!

The second factor in the rapid spread of conspiracy theories is technology. When I first became aware of US conspiracy theories in the 1970s, the type-generating computer was not affordable and the FAX had not been invented, photocopiers were expensive machines which still used rolls of coated paper, and newspapers and magazines were still set in metal type. There were a number of magazines discussing conspiracy theories - *Conspiracy Digest* I remember - but they were hard to find and had tiny circulations. Today, for a relatively small outlay, almost anybody can put their theories up on the Internet and wait for people to browse through them, pick them up and pass them on. Any old nonsense gets posted on the Net. There are no editors on your very own web page, no demands for evidence.

By far the most significant factor in the recent rise of conspiracy theories is the existence of real conspiracies in US history. People believe conspiracy theories because they see the world full of conspiracies. Before the early 1960s, had one been asked 'Who are American conspiracy theorists?' the answer would have been variations on a theme of the far right. It was elements on the far right who saw conspiracies to undermine America or promote blacks, and conspiracies by Jews, or bankers, or One Worlders. But American history since 1963 has provided prima facie evidence of political conspiracies:

- The assassination of John and Robert Kennedy, Martin Luther King, many of the Black Panther leadership, Malcolm X and Jimmy Hoffa;

- The shooting of Governor George Wallace when he appeared to threaten Richard Nixon's chances of winning the 1968 presidential election;

- The revelations in the 1960s of the various CIA operations run in the post-World War 2 years to influence world opinion;

- The Vietnam War and the massive domestic surveillance and disruption programmes by the FBI and CIA run against the opponents of that war;

- Watergate;

- In Watergate's aftermath, the revelation of CIA plots against foreign leaders;

- The CIA shipping opium in Laos and Vietnam;

- The revelation in the 1970s of the CIA's mind-control programmes, MK-Ultra, MK-Delta, etc.;

- Secret wars all around the world waged by the US or by proxies in the attempt to police global US interests and so on;

- And revelations of secret US government experiments on its citizens.

Since the advent of Republican governments in the 80s we've had Iran-Contra;[7] the October Surprise, the allegation that the Republicans did a deal with the Iranians holding American hostages that the hostages would be detained until after the 1980 American election to prevent Democratic President Carter having the electoral benefit of getting them released;[8] the clandestine arming of Iraq by Britain and America[9] and the subsequent operations to cover this up which in Britain involved major conspiracies to destroy companies and imprison witnesses;[10] billions of dollars ripped off from the American Savings and Loan banks; hundreds of thousands of corpses in Central America - including a few American nuns and a local Archbishop - courtesy of death squad regimes working as US proxy governments;[11] and everybody and their cousin running cocaine into the US by official permission of the CIA.[12]

We have had, in fact, what President Eisenhower warned America of in his farewell speech in 1960 - the military-industrial complex (with their intelligence agencies) running amok, totally beyond democratic control, gobbling up hundreds of billions of dollars. And we have had conspiracies, from every corner, day and night. The late Ralph J Gleason's *First Law of American Politics After Watergate* conveys this shift: 'no matter how paranoid you are what they are really doing is worse than you could possibly imagine.'

With Clinton and the Democrats in office, the Republican Party and its allies on the right have been churning out conspiracy theories about Clinton. Some of these, about his role while he was governor of the state, letting the CIA use facilities in Arkansas to run guns into Central America for the Contra war and bring cocaine back, seem to be true - at any rate are plausible and supported by evidence.[13] Many of the rest, the long lists of people alleged to have been killed covering up this or that conspiracy, I am unable to assess.[14] The paranoia about Clinton trying to engineer an American Reich, suspending elections and putting the US under UN control, strikes me as dotty in the extreme.[15] Some of it looks like political payback, the right having their revenge for the long line of Republican disasters beginning with Watergate and Nixon which were exploited - however incompetently - by the Democrats; and some of it, I would guess, is revenge by the US insurance companies whom Clinton had the temerity to challenge with his short-lived proposals for a system of government health insurance.[16]

Chris Carter, the writer/producer of *The X-Files* TV programme commented recently that his perception of the United States was formed by Watergate. But I would argue that the key event was a decade before that, with the killing of John F Kennedy, and the refusal of a handful of stubborn Americans to accept the official government line that Lee Harvey Oswald did it. If anybody is to be credited with starting the current mess we are in, it is those critics of the Warren Commission. Resisting all the government propaganda, personal vilification and manipulation by the media, their persistence destroyed the government's case, and made the first big hole in the official, Disney, version of America. From their research grew knowledge of the CIA and other US secret organisations; and without that knowledge the US media would not have known enough to investigate Watergate; and from there to do more investigations of the CIA, etc.

Fifty years of secrecy, lies, media manipulation and covert operations are coming back to bite the legs of the elite managers of American society and politics. The torrent of revelations since 1963 means that a large number of US citizens no longer believe US government statements about anything; and a significant minority believe their federal government capable of anything, up to and including planning to brainwash its citizenry (this is discussed below), detonating the bomb in Oklahoma to give itself a pretext for pushing draconian anti-terrorism laws through Congress, and even organising a secret conspiracy with extraterrestrial beings in the late 1940s.

So: why are we getting more conspiracy theories? It is at least partly the result of technology - computers, faxes and the Internet - and information overload, the whole thing buttressed by what I'm still willing to call the objective reality of US politics and imperialism.[17] Twenty years after *Close Encounters Of The Third Kind* and its still benign portrait of the human/extraterrestrial encounter, the makers of TV programmes like *The X-Files* and *Dark Skies* took all that UFO material and added bits of everything else that was floating around on the fringes of science, mysticism and the paranormal and fused it with the conspiracy theory strand in post-1963 American politics to produce a series of overlapping paranoid nightmares. The paranormal-conspiratorial fusion on which such programmes are built has three elements:

1. An acceptance of what used to be described as the paranormal or psychic as real, routine, operational.

2. Distrust of the US central government, chiefly, but of any government, in principal; a willingness to believe it capable of great evil and great secrecy - in short that it is a conspiracy against its citizens.

3. In particular the belief that there has been a massive US government cover-up of information on the UFO subject; and, possibly, a cover-up of contact between extraterrestrial beings and officials of the US government.

These elements were most comprehensively synthesised in the series *Dark Skies*, broadcast in this country on Channel Four, which rewrote some of the major events of US post-World War 2 history as if there really had been an on-going conspiracy between certain sections of the US government and aliens.

Twice before in American history in the 20th century 'aliens' were scapegoated. After World War 1 the 'aliens' were alleged socialist, anarchists and communist immigrants from Europe, who became the pretext for hysterical newspaper and political campaigns and the summary arrest of 10,000 people. After World War 2 a great 'communist conspiracy' was discovered, leading to the rise of Senator Joe McCar-

CFR a Trilet. com~!

thy and the 'ism' named after him. At the third great historical juncture for America, the end of the Cold War (and the loss of the external enemy justifying the massive expenditure on arms), when a sizeable populist minority (mostly on the right) were beginning to question the power of certain elites in American society, the entertainment industry began churning out nonsensical stories about alien-government conspiracies. These conspiracy theories do a number of things. First, while acknowledging the influence of elites in America, any impact this idea might have had is diluted by adding the alien conspiracy dimension. Second, as the 'communist threat' has vanished, a new external 'threat' - aliens from outer space - is being created and may, in a push, be used in the future to justify military programmes such as Star Wars. And third, in the case of *The X-Files*, the 'good guys' are presented as being... a group of agents and bureaucrats from America's internal security police, the FBI!

Notes

1. There are some examples in Kevin McClure's *Fortean Times Book Of The Millennium* (London: John Brown Publishing, 1996).

2. See *The Guardian*, 15 February 2000.

3. The claim that people are finding it harder to distinguish between fantasy and reality is difficult to sustain and is always pooh-poohed by the garbage media who claim that people know, for example, that the *Daily Sport* or the *National Inquirer* are not meant to be taken seriously. I am not so sure. A couple of years ago *The Sunday Telegraph* carried a story about a policeman in London who was psychic. The policeman concerned was quoted as saying, 'At first my colleagues in the police force thought it was all a bit odd. But since the BBC programme *The X-Files*, many have given it a lot more credence.' But *The X-Files* is fiction...

4. The teenage son of friends of mine began an Internet romance with an American girl. Eventually he went out to visit her in Kansas and was astonished to discover that in Kansas evolution is treated in the school system as having no more intellectual value than so-called 'creation science.'

5. See, for example, www.don-bradely.com for a list of supposed American 'concentration camps' and www.halfreepr@telepath.com

for the report of someone who visited many of the alleged 'concentration camps' and found... nothing. This has not prevented the 'concentration camp' story crossing over from the Net to print. Don Bradely's fantasies about the camps is in issue 3 of *The Truth Seeker* (PO Box 458, Devizes, SN10 1UJ.) These fantasies on the US right now regularly feature as the subject matter of American crime novels. A recent one is Donald Harstad's 'police procedural' *The Unknown Dead* (London: Fourth Estate, 1999).

6. One of the minority of books reporting unfriendly UFOs was Harold T Wilkins, *Flying Saucers On The Attack* (New York: Ace Books, 1954).

7. See Peter Dale Scott, Jonathan Marshall and Jane Hunter, *The Iran Contra Connection: Secret Teams And Covert Operations In The Reagan Era* (Boston: South End Press, 1987).

8. See Robert Parry, *Trick Or Treason: The October Surprise Mystery* (New York: Sheridan Square Press, 1993). Parry runs the Media Consortium, a radical (left radical) news agency, at www.consortiumnews.com

9. For an overall picture see Kenneth R Timmerman, *The Death Lobby: How The West Armed Iraq* (London: Fourth Estate, 1992). For the UK end, try John Sweeney, *Trading With The Enemy: Britain's Arming Of Iraq* (London: Pan, 1993).

10. Chris Cowley, *Guns, Lies And Spies* (London: Hamish Hamilton, 1992), Gerald James, *In The Public Interest* (London: Little,Brown, 1995) and David Leigh, *Betrayed: The Explosive Questions The Scott Inquiry Must Answer* (London: Bloomsbury, 1993).

11. On Central America, William Blum's *Killing Hope: US Military And CIA Interventions Since World War 2* (Monroe, Maine: Common Courage Press, 1995), is as good a place to start as any. Blum has a website at www.members.aol.com/bblum6/American_holocaust.htm. See also Robert Parry, *Lost History: Contras, Cocaine, The Press And 'Project Truth'* (Arlington: The Media Consortium, 1999).

12. See Peter Dale Scott and Jonathan Marshall, *Cocaine Politics: Drugs, Armies And The CIA In Central America* (Los Angeles: University of California Press, 1998). The Agency admitted in 1998 that it had been given political permission in 1982 to ignore the drug dealing

of people working for the Contras - in effect a 'get out of jail card' for any coke dealer willing to give a few thousand dollars to the Contras. See 'CIA Turned A Blind Eye To Contras Drug Smuggling' in *The Independent*, 7 November 1998. This uncomfortable fact has been largely ignored by the major American media - apparently because they had spent so long denying it to be true!

13. See, for example, Terry Reed and John Cummings, *Compromised: Clinton, Bush And The CIA*, (USA: Penmanin Books, 1995, ISBN 1883955025). There is also pretty substantial but not conclusive evidence that Clinton, while a Rhodes Scholar, had been recruited by the CIA to report on American students in the UK who opposed the war in Vietnam.

14. For example - one of many - the 1994 'Murder, Bank Fraud, Drugs And Sex' by Nick Guarino, editor of *The Wall Street Underground* - whatever that is! - which alleges 21 murders by the Clinton circle. On the phenomenon of the anti-Clinton stories being generated on the right, see Robert Parry, 'Dark Smears Of A Mean Machine' in *The Guardian*, 4 August 1994.

15. *Flashpoint, A Newsletter Ministry Of Texe Marrs*, June 1995, has as its page 1 headline, 'Fascist Terror Stalking America.' Marrs states, 'The destruction of the Reichstag in Berlin and the federal building in Oklahoma followed similar patterns. Both Hitler and Clinton cynically used the tragedies to justify Gestapo campaigns against their enemies... an evil clique of un-American money-hungry greedsters and murderers has grabbed the reins of such powerful groups as the CIA, FBI, DIA, DEA, DOD and BATF... ' Published by Living Truth Ministries, Austin, Texas. Love the bit about 'un-American money-hungry greedsters.'

16. The idea that since the Republicans are saying it about a Democratic president it must be false, has undoubtedly contributed to the American liberal left's inability to see what Bill Clinton actually is - the mouthpiece for the American global corporations whose members sponsored him in the Trilateral Commission. This is discussed below in chapter 4.

17. Looked at another way: here we are in Marshall McLuhan's global village; and what is village life like? Word of mouth, rumour, gossip - most of it inaccurate.

4. I Can't See Them But I Know They Are There

The most durable of the mega conspiracy theories is the anti-Jewish version. Though the persecution of Jews can be traced back to the beginning of recorded history, for the contemporary conspiracy-theory scene the starting point is the famous forgery by the Czarist secret police, *The Protocols Of The Learned Elders Of Zion*. The right have been distributing this preposterous forgery throughout the world for almost a century.[1] (It is a measure of the need racists have to hate somebody that they ever took this baloney seriously.) *The Protocols* was a particular spin on an established tradition - a genre - which explains political and social change by the activities of secret groups of conspirators, overlaid with hatred of Jews. That secret societies were believed to be powerful in 19th century Europe is not surprising. Most regimes were, or had recently been, monarchies; and most monarchies were run and policed by little groups of people round the King or Queen who faced constant opposition and plotting by rival groups. The ruling elite of 19th century Europe also had experience of secret societies of working men (forerunners of trade unions), masons, etc.; and threats to the established order were associated by the powers-that-be with secret societies. The memory of Madame Guillotine was still fresh in the collective mind of Europe's rulers.

The Jewish and Masonic fantasies of the 19th century merged with the post-World War 1 fear of Bolshevism that came to prominence after the 1917 Russian Revolution. As a result we got two things: the Communism-is-Jewish variant which survives, in little pockets, on the far right today; and the influential synthesis by the British writer Nesta Webster, who detected behind both French and Russian revolutions, the hand of an 18th century Masonic lodge, the Illuminati.[2]

While Webster's theory had a brief vogue in Britain in the 1920s - even Winston Churchill seems to have swallowed it, briefly - it really took root in the United States notably with the John Birch Society, which moved from a mainline, albeit extreme, anti-Communist viewpoint in the early 1950s, via Carroll Quigley's account of the Round Table network (discussed below), to a muddled view in which the Illuminati are mentioned but about whose actual role the Birchers remain a little vague.[3]

The John Birch Society and similar but smaller groups on the American far right, incorporated the 19th century belief in the threat of secret societies; the 1930s 'isolationist' beliefs that the US ought not to get embroiled in the evil, decadent ways of Europe; the anti-Communism which was the official ideology of the Western world for half a century; and fragments of real information about the elite planning bodies of Anglo-American (and later European and Japanese) capital. In the 1950s they identified the opposition as a 'Fabian, Rhodes Scholar, Zionist, Pinko, Communist, New Deal, Fair Deal, Socialist-minded gang.' [4] By 1997, with John Birch's adoption of the Illuminati and the group of theories which go under the heading of 'the New World Order,' this had become 'the Illuminati's Socialist/Communist/ Freemasonic New World Order.' [5] (As new information comes along it gets added on top, like layers of sediment.) Thus we get the contemporary American populist hostility to the United Nations and the more or less rationally explained belief that the US elite is planning to sacrifice the interests of ordinary Americans in pursuit of this elite's agenda.

This loosely-assembled conspiracy theory received a massive boost with the publication of Carroll Quigley's famous book *Tragedy And Hope* in 1966 which revealed the existence of the Round Table network, set up with Cecil Rhodes' money just before and just after World War 1.[6] The revelation of this network, and especially of its links to its US branch, the Council on Foreign Relations (CFR), seemed to offer the proof of the great conspiracy - if not quite the conspiracy the US radical right was expecting. For while the radical right was aware of the CFR and the Rhodes Scholar programme, they had not connected them. Quigley did that: Quigley seemed to join up the dots.

For noticing the significance of Quigley when the establishment had closed ranks to freeze out Quigley's book,[7] we owe thanks to the radical right. For Quigley is the starting point for the examination of the influence of elite groups on Anglo-American-European history. The sequence of events is this. In the beginning (1908-1920) Cecil Rhodes' money created the Round Table groups in the British Commonwealth, the Royal Institute for International Affairs (Chatham House) in London, the Council on Foreign Relations (CFR) in the US, and the various branches of the Institute of Pacific Affairs. Quigley does not actually provide the evidence for these claims but even a casual skim through the conventional literature on the period shows that these claims are basically correct.[8] These events took place when Britain was still - just - top dog in the world; and this network of what would now be called think-tanks and political action groups tried to formulate and implement foreign policies which would (a) benefit Britain and America and (b) move the world in the direction Rhodes sought - towards an Anglo-American dominated commonwealth of nations. (The term commonwealth came from the Round Table people.)[9]

By the end of World War 2, when the US had supplanted the UK as the world's leading imperial power, the British dominance of this network was over. During the war the Council on Foreign Relations (CFR) planned the expansion of the US empire in the post-World War 2 years without discussing it with its UK counterpart. Although allies with Britain in the war against the Axis powers, elements of American business and the government spent the war planning how to get their hands on the British Empire after it.[10]

The CFR has dominated the ranks of the US foreign service for most of the post-World War 2 period: on that the US 'radical right,' the elite conspiracy theorists, are correct. As the Internet site *roundtable* endlessly demonstrates, virtually all the foreign policy managers of America in the post-World War 2 world have been members of the CFR.[11] But it is not clear to me that this tells us anything, any more than the fact that their UK equivalents, almost without exception, will have attended Oxford or Cambridge University.

In the early post-World War 2 years other groups of elite managers were formed. One was the Bilderberg group, begun in 1954 by the Polish éminence grise Joseph Retinger, probably - though not provably - working for the British secret service, and funded by the CIA. For almost 30 years Bilderberg was simply not reported on by the major Anglo-American media. One British journalist who tried to write about the group in his column in the *Financial Times*, Gordon Tether, had those columns pulled from the paper, eventually lost his job after 20 years, and ended up publishing the columns which the *FT* refused to print, including three on Bilderberg, in a little pamphlet.[12]

Although the major media on both sides of the Atlantic have continued by and large to accept the Bilderberg's requests to be not reported, it has been reported on in the USA in a magazine called *The Spotlight* for over a decade.[13] In the current climate of slightly greater openness,

47

* One of those instances when R's leftism gets in the way of him accepting someone else's conspiracy theory

one of Bilderberg's recent guests, Tony Blair, belatedly included his visit to a recent Bilderberg conference in his Parliamentary declaration of interests but only after an initial parliamentary answer denying that he had attended the meeting. Asked by the Conservative MP Christopher Gill which members of his government had attended meetings of the Bilderberg Group, Blair - or his office - replied in a written answer on 16 March 1998, 'None.' In fact as well as Blair, Gordon Brown and George Robertson had attended Bilderberg meetings. Even more interestingly, I was informed by Bilderberg's administrator that the late John Smith was on the Bilderberg Steering Group from 1989 to 1992. Smith's role in the inner council of Bilderberg sits uneasily with the public image of Smith as the genial, honest, Scots, Old Labour, lawyer.[14]

In the last couple of years, apparently in response to stories about the group on the Net, Bilderberg has ceased to be quite as secretive as it used to be and a couple of major British newspapers, *The Mail On Sunday* and *The Scotsman*, have published pieces - albeit not very good pieces - about the group. In late 1999, for the first time in the group's existence, the minutes of that year's meeting were leaked, extracts were published in the magazine *The Big Issue*, and the whole document was posted on the Internet.[15] This remarkable event was not recorded by any of the British media. It was apparently not a story. (No clearer indication of the influence of Bilderberg could be asked for, really, than its ability to persuade the entire major British media to ignore those minutes...)[16]

As the post-World War 2 capitalist world changed, notably with the emergence of Japan as a major economic power, members of the American Council on Foreign Relations formed the Trilateral Commission in the 1970s, consisting of representatives of the United States, Europe and, for the first time, Japan.[17]

Why The Right?

The strange thing about all this is the fact that the Anglo-American left is basically not interested in these elite management or power elite groups. Despite the groups being composed entirely of the major figures from world capital and politics - the left's enemy, opposition, target group - somehow the left finds this of little interest. Apart from that brief flutter of interest in the late 1970s when Trilateralist Jimmy

Carter became president of the US, the Anglo-American left has passed on these groups, leaving them to the right.

Why it has happened that it is chiefly the right which is interested in mega conspiracies in general and these elite groups in particular, is not clear to me. In part this is the result of this subject becoming 'contaminated' for those on the left by the interest in it expressed by the far right.[18] In other words, such is the left's fear of being linked with the right, anything the right takes up immediately becomes 'untouchable' to the left.

It was the powers-that-be in 19th century Europe who were first attracted to ideas of conspiracy to explain the uprising of their citizens against them; and to some extent the survival of the mega conspiracy theory into the 21st century is simply an historical anachronism. But such theories' survival has certainly been assisted by almost a century of official propaganda by the state about the reality of a vast Soviet conspiracy; and having believed it, the right did not find it so hard to accept the reality of other conspiracies.

The radical right has two distinct views.

1. What we might call the hard-core view is of hidden forces running the world - the classic mega conspiracy theories. False though most of the popular versions of this are, it is not possible to simply say they will always be false. There are honest-to-goodness secret societies in the contemporary world: think of the Masons (especially the Italian version, P2), Opus Dei, and the Knights of Malta, for starters.[19] Recently there has been interest in the Yale University-based secret society, Skull and Bones.[20] In Britain the Masons have local influence in certain sections of society, notably the police and local government.[21] In Italy, P2 even acquired national power for a while.[22] And if we did not know about P2 in the 1970s, we could be equally unaware of its equivalent today...

2. The soft-core view of the right is something like this: it perceives transnational forces seeking to undermine the nation state and/or the status quo. This is sort of correct: there are indeed globalising forces trying to diminish the nation state. The world capitalist system is regulated - in theory, any way - by institutions, the International Monetary Fund, the World Bank and the World Trade Organisation, which are dominated by Americans, which represent the interests of the big cor-

porations - most of them American. Transnational corporations do not like nation states because nation states are one of the few organisations capable of opposing them. The policies of organisations like the IMF or World Trade Organisation are formulated, in part, at gatherings of the world's elite such as Bilderberg and the Trilateral Commission.[23] But having correctly identified them as significant, the right has fundamentally misinterpreted these elite discussion groups as the master controllers - the Executive Committees - of the capitalist universe, bent on subjugating the entire globe to their plans for a New World Order. The evidence suggests that the CFR, Bilderberg, Trilateral, etc. do not, in fact, generally pull the levers but merely set agendas and try to produce a consensus.[24] But at least the right takes these groups seriously. The transatlantic left - and the major media - mostly ignores them, even when their members look as though they are running things.

The EU

Take the European Union. Romano Prodi, now president of the European Commission, was a Steering Committee Member of the Bilderberg Group in the 80s. Prodi has limited the declarations of interests required of his Commissioners to the last 10 years, something not done in the previous Commissions, and so has avoided declaring his Bilderberg role in the 1980s. Prodi's 20 Commissioners include 7 other identified members of the elite management groups:

- Mario Monti, Steering Committee member of Bilderberg (1983-1993); member of the Executive committee of the Trilateral Commission Europe, from 1988 to 1997.

- Pedro Solbes Mira, Trilateral Commission since 1996; Bilderberg 1999.

- Chris Patten, Trilateral Commission.

- Gunther Verheugen, Bilderberg 1995.

- Antonio Vitorino, Bilderberg 1996.

- Erikki Liikanen, Bilderberg 1999.

- Frits Bolkestein, Member of the Royal Institute of International Affairs, Chatham House, in London; Bilderberg 1996.[25]

From its inception the European Union was the creation of the elite with the notional bits of democracy - the talking-shop parliament and elections to it - added later.[26] Pro-European Union Hugo Young's recent history of Britain's relationship with the EEC/European Union,[27] describes in great detail the conspiracy by a section of the British state to get Britain into the EEC/EU. Young seems to think he has diminished or made ironic the conspiratorial aspects of this with his book's title, *This Blessed Plot*. In fact, from the most official of sources - the hitherto secret Foreign Office account of the negotiations with the EEC/EU - he describes a conspiracy by a group of politicians and officials, led by the Foreign Office, to deceive the British people. Everything the British Eurosceptics have claimed for the last twenty years is confirmed - and then some.

For example, the European Movement was one of the organisations funded by the CIA in the 1950s in Uncle Sam's search for reliable anti-Soviet alliances.[28] The Cold War was fought largely as a series of clandestine conspiracies by both sides. Each reported to its populace the conspiracies of its opponents - not its own. American and British attempts to penetrate Soviet airspace on intelligence missions led to shooting encounters in which hundreds of people died, which were never reported in Britain or America.[29] In the 1950s the Americans made attempts to control a huge chunk of the non-Communist world. By the mid-1950s they had made major inroads into Western European trade unions[30] and the CIA was running a massive propaganda operation, centred round the organisation called the Congress for Cultural Freedom.[31]

Other programmes existed to influence public opinion in Britain. Sympathetic Brits visited America on schemes that included Harkness, Fulbright and Kennedy scholarships; various Congressional programmes, the Smith-Mundt scholarships, Eisenhower Exchange Fellowships, and the State Department's Young Leader programme (which embraced Roy Hattersley and Margaret Thatcher). In 1983 newly-elected MP Tony Blair took the American freebie trip.

Another set of organisations have promoted the Anglo-American alliance: the British Atlantic Committee, the Atlantic Council, the British North-American Committee, the British Atlantic Group of Young Politicians, the Atlantic Education Trust, the Atlantic Information Centre for Teachers, the Standing Conference of Atlantic Organisations, the Trade Union Committee for European and Transatlantic Understanding, and who knows which others you would find if you had a thorough hunt. These Anglo-American bodies presumably have counterparts in all the other NATO countries as well as other countries with which the US is allied, though I know of no systematic research on them. Generally such bodies are only visible to the public during periods of crisis. When the New Zealand government in the early 1980s tried to enforce a 'no nuclear ships' policy on the US Navy, the New Zealand-America network was suddenly worthy of interest to the New Zealand media as the US began leaning on the Kiwi government.[32]

The organisation of most current interest in Britain is the Trade Union Committee for European and Transatlantic Understanding (TUCETU). This began as the Labour Committee on Transatlantic Understanding in the 1970s, founded by Joseph Godson, US Labour Attaché at the US embassy in London in the 1950s, who talent-spotted and promoted among the British Labour movement. Currently organised by two officials of the NATO-financed Atlantic Council, TUCETU incorporated Peace Through NATO, the group central to Conservative Defence Secretary Michael Heseltine's Ministry of Defence campaign against CND in the early 1980s, and receives over £100,000 a year from the Foreign Office. TUCETU chair Alan Lee Williams was a Labour defence minister in the Callaghan Government before he defected to the SDP; director Peter Robinson runs the National Union of Teachers' education centre at Stoke Rochford near Grantham. In the mid-1980s Williams and Robinson were members of the European policy group of the Washington Centre for Strategic and International Studies.

The Atlantic Council/TUCETU network provided New Labour's Ministry of Defence team. The initial Defence Secretary, George Robertson, now head of NATO, was a member of the Council of the Atlantic Committee from 1979 to 90; Lord Gilbert, Minister of State for Defence Procurement, is listed as TUCETU vice-chair; and MoD press office biographical notes on junior Defence Minister John Speller state that he 'has been a long standing member of the Trade Union Committee for European and Transatlantic Understanding.' [33]

Is Ramsay making something of all this yet?

BAP

The latest in the long line of American-funded groups seeking to keep the British ruling elite pro-American began life as the British American Project for the Successor Generation, and is now just known as the British-American Project, or BAP for short. You may not have heard about BAP because the major media in Britain have mostly ignored it in the same way they mostly ignore the Ditchley Foundation,[34] the CFR, Bilderberg and the Trilateral Commission. But BAP organises large annual gatherings, runs a UK and US office and publishes a newsletter, albeit one to which you and I cannot subscribe. In this newsletter BAP members are kept up to date about the career developments of other BAP members. The BAP newsletter's message is clear enough: stick with us, boys and girls, and you will go far. After the 1997 election the BAP newsletter headline was 'Big Swing To BAP' as it celebrated the arrival of five BAP alumni in the Labour government: namely Marjorie Mowlam, Chris Smith, Peter Mandelson, George Robertson and Elizabeth Symons. Other senior Labour figures to have been involved with BAP are: Jonathan Powell, Blair's chief of staff; Geoff Mulgan, now in the Downing Street Policy Unit; and Matthew Taylor, some time Head of Policy at Labour Party HQ.[35]

The BAP is interesting but not exceptional, nor probably terribly influential. These groups are not centrally about conspiratorial manipulation of policy but maintaining the Atlanticist view, the kind of instinctive pro-American, pro-NATO consensus which is so powerful in this country, that as soon as you stray from it *Newsnight* anchorman Jeremy Paxman's eyebrow rises and his voice gives the viewers the cue that, yes, this person is not to be taken seriously. Paxman, coincidentally, has been on a BAP jamboree.

Like the Round Table, the Council on Foreign Relations, Ditchley, Wilton Park,[36] and Chatham House, the BAP is not so much a secret organisation, as a discreet organisation. This tradition of discreet, publicity-averse, elite gatherings will continue so long as the British and American elite find them useful ways of agreeing an agenda, building networks and getting their views across without the impedance of the electorate and democracy. Equally such groupings will continue to be the subject of conspiracy theorising so long as they continue to look like conspiracies; and they will continue to look like conspiracies so long as the rest of us are kept in the dark about their activities.

The Official Conspiracy Theory

There is one obvious exception to the official prohibition on interest in conspiracies. Since 1918 until fairly recently we have all been officially encouraged to believe in the existence of one conspiracy, the Red Menace. In post-World War 2 Britain the most important and successful conspiracy theorists were the cold warriors who pumped out endless stories of Soviet espionage and subversion in this country since the war. These reached some kind of climax in the 1974-77 period when a number of large-scale disinformation projects were mounted by the Anglo-American intelligence services against the labour movement, the Labour Party and Harold Wilson in particular, claiming that the Red Menace was taking over Britain. Mrs Thatcher was one of those who believed the cold warriors' tales of the Soviet menace in Britain. She looked at the Trades Union Congress and saw Moscow subversion - 'the enemy within.' On the basis of nothing more than the fact that Labour Prime Minister Harold Wilson made a number of visits to the Soviet Union during the Cold War, like many others in her circle on the right of the Tory Party at the time, Mrs Thatcher suspected that Harold Wilson was a KGB agent - and believed this strongly enough to voice this to a very senior civil servant in the administration of Wilson's successor, James Callaghan.[37] In her belief in the reality of the Soviet 'threat' she was tutored in the mid-1970s, after becoming leader of the Tory Party, by a group of cold warriors, including perhaps the most important of them all, Brian Crozier.[38] Crozier had worked for much of the post-World War 2 period for the CIA and a British state propaganda and disinformation organisation called the Information Research Department (IRD) whose chief function was to propagate the official Communist conspiracy theory.[39]

To ensure that we believed in the reality of this approved conspiracy theory, the Anglo-American intelligence services - outstanding examples of institutionalised conspiracies in the 20th century - have spent a ton of money propagating it while denigrating anybody who turned up with any other kind of conspiracy. This hypocrisy reached some kind of peak in 1967 when the CIA - a vast worldwide conspiracy - put out a message to all its stations and personnel about the Kennedy assassination. By 1967 the first wave of critics of the Warren Commission - notably Mark Lane and Edward Epstein - had appeared and were getting attention, especially abroad. The instruction from CIA HQ in Langley, Virginia, was that CIA personnel were to use their political and media assets to put out the line that the kind of conspiracy described by the Warren Commission critics could not possibly exist!

Three years before this comic event, the CIA's formal relationship with the Warren Commission investigating JFK's assassination was handled by the late James Jesus Angleton, head of CIA counter-intelligence even though - or because! - Angleton's department was deeply embroiled in the mysterious goings-on in Mexico City into which Oswald wandered.[40] Having been conned by his friend, Kim Philby and aware, via the Venona decrypts of Soviet wartime radio communications, of the scale of Soviet espionage in America during the war,[41] Angleton became increasingly, and many would say disablingly, paranoid. Angleton believed, among other things, that the split between the Soviet and Chinese Communist Parties in the 1960s (up to and including a shooting war on their borders) was a disinformation campaign to lull the West into a false sense of security.[42] There are people on the fringe on the UK-US intelligence services who believed for years after the fall of the Soviet empire that the whole thing - demolishing the Berlin Wall and all - was a deception operation!

Which proves what, I am not entirely sure. It certainly shows that people in the grip of theories find it difficult to change their minds: the human brain is adept at finding reasons why information which refutes our core beliefs can be ignored. It may also demonstrate that of all theories, conspiracy theories, once internalised, can be the most difficult to shed. For, by their very nature, conspiracy theories have built into them strategies for accommodating information which apparently contradicts them. After a recent piece in the local newspaper about me in which I was foolish enough to talk about this field, a man came to see me claiming that he was a kind of robot: all his actions were controlled by some outside body. I knew he was a nutter almost immediately - a belief which was confirmed a little later in the conversation when he began telling me how some people (unspecified) had broken into his flat, removed his penis and substituted a smaller one. 'Oh boy!' thought I, but I continued patiently trying to pick his preposterous story to pieces. At one point I obviously had made some kind of impact for he began to speculate that I would say these things, wouldn't I, if I were part of the group controlling him...

Notes

1. *The Protocols* have been debunked many times. I have a 1938 version, John Gwyer, *Portraits Of Mean Men: A Short History Of The 'Protocols Of The Elders Of Zion,'* (Bristol: Cobden-Sanderson, 1938). The standard text is Norman Cohn, *Warrant For Genocide: The Myth Of The Jewish World Conspiracy And The Protocols Of The Elders Of Zion*, (Harmondsworth: Penguin, 1967).

2. On Nesta Webster see Richard Gilman, *Behind World Revolution: The Strange Career Of Nesta H Webster*, (Ann Arbor: Insight Books, 1982). Roberts, see chapter 1, note 12, discusses the little that is known about the Illuminati.

3. See for example Gary Allen and Larry Abraham *None Dare Call It Conspiracy*, and Abraham's update, *Call It Conspiracy*, both cited in chapter 1, note 11. Abraham can't quite shake the old Illuminati habit and quotes (p.257) the Illuminati's alleged founder Weishaupt, and states, 'Weishaupt's strategy still holds.' Which is a long way from saying the Illuminati are the conspiracy behind the conspiracies.

4. Cited on p.77 of George Thayer, *The Farther Shore Of Politics* (London: Allan Lane/Penguin, 1968).

5. Description in a 1997 US newsletter from evangelical Christian David Smith of Waxahachie, Texas.

6. Macmillan (US) 1966 originally but now republished by several organisations on the US right. To my knowledge Quigley was discussed first outside the far right in the UK in Robert Eringer, *The Global Manipulators* (Bristol: Pentacle, 1980). In the early 1980s I loaned Eringer my copy of the LaRouche book *Dope Inc!* Robert, if you read this, I still want it back!

7. It seems to have attracted only two tiny reviews in the *Virginia Quarterly Review*, Spring 1966, and *Annals Of The American Academy Of Political And Social Science*, November 1966.

8. I discussed this in a piece in *Lobster* 1, which I reprinted in number 25 with the arrival of Bill Clinton as a president who spoke publicly of his admiration for Quigley, one of his tutors at university. His comments about Quigley generated delirious fantasies on the far right but - alas? - it was clear from those comments that Clinton had never come across Quigley's two books on the 20th century ruling elite and

was not, as the far right hoped, acknowledging his (Clinton's) role as the stooge of the Round Table-Fabian-One World conspiracy!

9. Rhodes actually dreamed of reuniting Britain and its former colony, America, and one of the American end of the Round Table network, Clarence Streit, argued the case for this in *Union Now* (London: Right Book Club, 1939) and *Union Now With Britain* (London: Jonathan Cape, 1941). This idea still has echoes today in the idea, current in some sections of the anti-EU Conservative Party and some areas of the City of London, that Britain should join up with the US in a North American Free Trade Area, rather than proceed further into a federal European Union.

10. See Laurence H Shoup and William Minter, *Imperial Brain Trust* (London & New York: Monthly Review Press, 1977) for an account of the wartime planning for the post-World War 2 era by study groups set up by the Council on Foreign Relations.

11. www.geocities.com/CapitolHill/2807

12. *The Banned Articles Of C Gordon Tether*, C Gordon Tether (ISBN 00905821009).

13. *The Spotlight* documents the US-dominated elite groups like Bilderberg while offering its readers the anti-Jewish conspiracy theory it detects beneath the New World Order.

14. In 1992 he became leader of the Labour Party.

15. *The Scotsman*, 11 May 1998and *The Mail On Sunday* (Night and Day section), 14 June 1998. Best single article on the Bilderbergers is Mike Peters, 'Bilderberg And The Origins Of The EU' in *Lobster* 32 (December 1996). This is among the material on the Bilderberg at Tony Gosling's site www.tlio.demon.co.uk/report.htm. The first book published in this country outside the far right to discuss the group was Robert Eringer's *The Global Manipulators* - see note 6 above. On the far right it was the subject of a chapter in National Front founder A K Chesterton's *The New Unhappy Lords*, (Hampshire: Candour Publishing, 4th edition, 1975). The 1999 Bilderberg minutes were posted at www.schnews.org.uk/bilderberg/index/html

16. By using 'persuade' here I am not suggesting that Bilderberg rang around the media and shut it down, though that may have happened. My suspicion would be that self-censorship rather than censor-

ship is the order of the day. Why write a story which you know your editor is not going to be interested in?

17. The Trilateral Commission's website is at www.trilateral.org/. On the history of the organisation - and more on the Bilderberg group - see Holly Sklar (ed.) *Trilateralism* (Boston: South End Press, 1980). Among the Trilateral Commission's members in the early 1970s was the then young, largely unknown Governor of Georgia, Jimmy Carter. Among the Trilateral Commission members in the 1980s was the, then largely unknown, young Governor of Arkansas, William Jefferson Clinton.

18. The idea of ideological or political 'contamination' was first expressed by Mike Peters in his essay 'Bilderberg And The Origins Of The EU' in *Lobster* 32. This is on the web at www.bilderberg.org/bildhist.htm

19. Opus Dei is formally described as an ultra-conservative organisation for lay Catholics but looks like a secret society to most people. There is no thorough study of the organisation to my knowledge but in 1998 a former member, Maria del Carmen Tapia, published an exposé in America, *Beyond The Threshold*. See 'Catholic Group Is Accused Of Brainwashing' in *The Daily Telegraph*, 21 September 1998 p.7. See also 'The Don Who Unmasked A Secret Sect' in *The Sunday Times*, 18 January 1981 p.15 and 'The "Holy Mafia" Under Attack' in *The Daily Telegraph*, 8 April 1986.

The most reliable article on the Knights of Malta is Françoise Hervet, 'The Sovereign Military Order Of Malta' in *Covert Action Information Bulletin* 25 (Winter 1986).

An early example of an attempt to deal rationally with this fuzzy area is in Jonathan Marshall's essay 'Brief Notes On The Political Importance Of Secret Societies' originally published in Marshall's short-lived *Parapolitics USA* and republished in *Lobster* 5 & 6, 1984.

20. See the essay on this at www.parascope.com/articles/0997/skull-bones.htm and the section in Jonathan Vanakin's *Conspiracies, Cover-ups And Crimes* (New York: Dell, 1992). Quite how secret Skull and Bones actually is is unclear to me. Any visitor to Yale University can see the Skull and Bones headquarters in a large building in the centre of the campus.

21. See Martin Short, *Inside The Brotherhood* (London: Grafton Books, 1989), for many British examples.

22. On P2 see Philip Willan, *Puppet Masters: The Political Use Of Terrorism In Italy* (London: Constable, 1991).

23. On the Trilateral Commission, see Stephen Gill, *American Hegemony And The Trilateral Commission* (Cambridge: Cambridge University Press, 1990).

24. These ideas, now widespread on the US populist and Christian right, have penetrated as far as former Republican presidential candidate, the Reverend Pat Robertson. Robertson's 1991 book articulating some of this was the subject of two long articles expressing shock and incredulity at this fact in the *New York Review Of Books*, 2 February 1995 and 20 April 1995.

25. This section on the elite affiliations of EU commissioners is a summary of an article in *Lobster* 38. Most of the information on the affiliations of the Commissioners came from their declarations of interest.

26. There are now said to be 10,000 lobbyists in Brussels working at the European Commission and Parliament. See Balanya, Doherty, Hoedeman, Man'anit and Wesselius, *Europe Inc.* (London: Pluto, 2000), p.3.

27. *This Blessed Plot* (London: Macmillan, 1998).

28. See Steve Weissman, Phil Kelly and Mark Hosenball, 'The CIA Backs The Common Market' in Philip Agee and Louis Woolf (eds) *Dirty Work: The CIA In Western Europe* (London: Zed Press, 1978).

29. See Paul Lashmar, *Spy Flights Of The Cold War* (Stroud, Glos.: Sutton, 1996).

30. This subject has yet to be documented fully but see Anthony Carew, *Labour Under The Marshall Plan* (Manchester: Manchester University Press, 1987) for examples of the US operations in the immediate post-World War 2 era.

31. Subject of a large recent book, Frances Stonor Saunders, *Who Paid The Piper?* (London: Granta, 1999). For more details of the propaganda war waged by the US in the post-1945 era see Scott Lucas,

Freedom's War: The US Crusade Against The Soviet Union 1945-56
(Manchester: Manchester University Press, 1999).

32. See chapter 5 of Paul Rogers and Paul Landais-Stamp, *Rocking The Boat: New Zealand, The United States And The Nuclear-Free Zone Controversy In The 1980s* (Oxford: Berg, 1989).

33. This section of TUCETU is taken from David Osler's 'American And Tory Intervention In The British Unions Since The 1970s' in *Lobster* 33.

34. A British organisation which hosts meetings of the Anglo-American and European political elites at Ditchley Park.

35. For the details of BAP membership see the essay by Tom Easton in *Lobster* 33. A shorter version of the same information is in John Pilger, *Hidden Agendas* (London: Vintage, 1998) pp.96-7.

36. Another British site of meetings of the elite, funded by the Foreign Office. See Dexter M Keezer, *A Unique Contribution To International Relations: The Story Of Wilton Park*, (Maidenhead, Berkshire: Macgraw-Hill, 1973).

37. Kenneth O Morgan, *Callaghan: A Life* (Oxford: Oxford University Press, 1997) p.610. The 1974-77 operations are discussed in detail in Stephen Dorril and Robin Ramsay, *Smear! Wilson And The Secret State* (London: Fourth Estate, 1991).

38. On his meetings with Thatcher and his intelligence career, see his memoir *Free Agent* (London: HarperCollins, 1995).

39. See Paul Lashmar and James Oliver, *Britain's Secret Propaganda War 1948-1977* (Stroud, Glos.: Sutton, 1998). IRD was formally attached to the Foreign Office but grew in the 1950s and early 60s into a self-sustaining bureaucracy running its own policies.

40. See Peter Dale Scott, *Deep Politics II: Essays On Oswald, Mexico And Cuba* (Skokie, Illinois: Green Archive Publications, 1995).

41. The Venona decrypts were tape recordings of radio traffic between the Soviet Embassy in the US and Moscow during the war. Moscow thought them unbreakable but was wrong. The US slowly broke a proportion of them and so learned of the extensive Soviet espionage network in the US. But this knowledge was kept secret until recently. See, for example John Earl Haynes and Harvey Klehr,

Venona: Decoding Soviet Espionage In America (London: Yale University Press, 1999) and Allan Weinstein and Alexander Vassiliev, *The Haunted Wood* (New York. Random House, 1999).

42. On Angleton see the biography by Tom Mangold, *Cold Warrior* (London· Simon and Schuster, 1991).

5. It's The State, Dummy

In both the UK and the USA the military-intelligence complex, the national security state created during the Cold War, works in secrecy and depends on secrecy for its survival in its current bloated form. This is obviously much more true of the UK: the US does have more systems of democratic oversight; for all its faults, it still has a less forelock-tugging print media than we do (would the British press have uncovered Watergate?); and even though the Freedom of Information legislation is being watered down, it still produces astonishing material.[1] There remains a huge, secret, national security state in this country, beyond political control. This was clearly demonstrated by the story that between them MI5 and MI6 spent £200 (!) over budget on their new headquarters in London.[2] Despite the fact that all the great British traitors of the past century were professional intelligence officers, mere politicians are deemed not reliable enough to be given access to 'the secret world.' In a sense the entire secret apparatus of the modern state - military, policing, intelligence and security organisations - are simply state conspiracies; and all too frequently are conspiracies directed against the taxpayers who fund them.[3]

MI5 currently claim to employ around 2000 people full-time. You may wonder what they are doing now they do not have the Soviet Trade Mission to keep them busy. Working against terrorism, organised crime and drugs, apparently. MI5 tell us they no longer have anyone keeping an eye on British subversives. Or is it that they have simply redefined the subversives as terrorists? In either case, how would we know? With the exception of the identity of the last two MI5 Director Generals, the rest of their work and their personnel is officially secret. At any rate secret to us, until someone blows the whistle, something goes wrong; or, as in recent years, bureaucratic turf wars break out with other government agencies, in the most spectacular recent case, with the police.

MI5's struggle with the police over drugs and organised crime in the early 1990s provoked both sides to engage in a war of leaking to, and briefing of, the media. MI5 tried to show their political masters what a clever, efficient organisation they are, and why they should be given this or that role; and the police tried to show that it was dangerous to give this unaccountable organisation these areas. (As if the police were accountable!) MI5 were bound to win - and they did. At the end of this media war MI5 had been awarded part of the drugs and organised crime franchises. Have the prices of heroin and cocaine risen since MI5 got involved? No, they have fallen. (Re: the war on drugs. The drugs have won.)

The investigation of these state organisations and their activities, which is essentially conspiracy research, but which is more often called parapolitics, takes the official account of reality and makes the world more complex. 400 books, half a dozen journals, who knows how many websites or how many million pages of declassified material from the FBI and CIA on the Kennedy assassination alone have generated immense, almost unmanageable complexity.[4] This is replicated, albeit to a much lesser extent, in many of the big political scandals of the last twenty years. The documentation on the Iran-Contra affair, for example, or the story of the British state's covert operations against the IRA, or the clandestine arming of Iraq, is now vast.

If conspiracy research complicates things, conspiracy theories simplify reality. The chaos of the world's economic system is reduced to a cabal of Jewish bankers. The US were in Vietnam because of the heroin in the Golden Triangle; or was there at the behest of Howard Hughes so he could sell more helicopters. America is awash with drugs because of a Communist conspiracy by the Soviets and/or Chinese to undermine America. Britain is in economic decline because the KGB runs the unions which are ruining Britain. The British Empire was lost because it was undermined by a conspiracy of Communist traitors. And so forth. This simplification is undoubtedly part of the appeal of conspiracy theories. The world's ills are explained by the actions of this or that group or individual, and all the difficult, time-consuming complexity of real life, real politics - and real conspiracies! - melts away.

Mega conspiracy theories are simply bad theories, held irrationally. Lyndon LaRouche and his followers have no evidence that the Queen runs the world's heroin traffic. There is no evidence that a secret Masonic cabal called the Illuminati have been running the world since the late 18th century. (There is almost no evidence that the Illuminati ever existed...) There is no evidence that the world's financial system is controlled by Jewish bankers. There is no evidence of a US government-alien conspiracy which began in the late 1940s. Most mega conspiracy theories barely deserve the description of 'theory' at all and are merely absurd allegations.

The difficulty is that in a sense the people who are currently producing and recycling all the rubbish about global or mega conspiracies, the David Ickes and William Coopers[5] of this world, are right. But only in a sense. Some of the world's politics and economics is influenced - but not controlled - by little groups of people. There are bankers ripping us off - but few of them are Jewish. A friend of mine attended a conference of bankers in New York which was addressed by a big cheese from the US Federal Reserve who began his talk thus: 'Ladies and gentlemen, between us we control two thirds of the world's capital...' The Bilderberg Group does exist, does meet. The Trilateral Commission does exist, does discuss a new world order. After all, those attending such gatherings are the guardians and managers of transnational capital, and disorder is what they do not want (it is bad for profits). They may not want the New World Order of the paranoid fantasists but they certainly want order of some kind.

Mega conspiracy theories are amusing - for a while. Unfortunately their chief result is to enable the powers-that-be to dismiss people doing research into real conspiracies along with those who believe that the Jews, the Illuminati, aliens, or shape-shifting reptiles[6] are running the world. David Icke and the many Americans from whom he has adopted these ideas, pollute the subject matter, unwittingly playing into the hands of the very people they think they are opposing. The 'Jewish banking conspiracy' nonsense has served for half a century in this country to make people nervous about researching the political power of finance capital in this society. The absurd allegations floating around the so-called 'underground' press in the late 1960s and early 1970s, that US policy in Vietnam was being run to benefit the heroin trade, tended to discredit serious research in this area, notably Alfred McKoys' work on the role of US personnel in shipping opium for some of the mountain tribes who had been recruited to fight against the Vietcong.[7] The Illuminati nonsense makes academics and journalists dubious about the alleged influence of real groups such as Bilderberg.

David Icke

David Icke is now the most prominent British conspiracy theorist. His journey from Green Party activist to global conspiracy theorist has been one of the stranger journeys in recent years. In its oddity it is only matched, perhaps, by that of Lyndon LaRouche Jnr. who moved from being the leader of a US Trotskyist splinter group to global conspiracy theorist with the British Royal Family at the heart of his theories. I have tried and failed to read two of Icke's books - they are unreadable dreck - but I have seen an early video recording of David talking in a Liverpool theatre in the mid-1990s. Even then Icke drew several hundred people, who paid to see him. Icke strides round the stage, he lines up all our discontents, lists all the terrible things that are being done to the planet - the green element in his thinking - and discusses the catastrophe approaching. That takes about fifteen minutes and, yes, for an apolitical, mainstream audience, he does it rather well. He was a well-known TV personality, after all: he's real, good-looking and TV-legitimised. He then asks the audience, not "What is the cause or causes of this?," but "Who is behind this?" Once you ask that question you're off into uncharted territory. His answer then - his views have changed since - was a mishmash of American conspiracy theories about semi-clandestine groups like the Trilateral Commission (discussed below) and the Council on Foreign Relations; a smattering of ufology's greatest hits - Majestic 12, the alleged alliance with the Greys; and old chestnuts like the Illuminati. Icke has continued the great American conspiracy tradition of adding new mega conspiracy theories to the old ones. The conspiracy with the extraterrestrials does not falsify or discredit the theory about the conspiracy by the Illuminati. Just add it on - the more the merrier! This makes life simple, of course, for audiences who are not used to handling evidence. The audience do not have to make the effort to decide if theory X has falsified and supplanted theory Y. All they have to do is add it to the list.

But Icke's ideas have changed recently. The American writer on things conspiratorial, the late Jim Keith, wrote of Icke's latest book, *The Biggest Secret: The Book That Will Change the World*: 'Icke's new book is a classic... a huge, detailed, riotous excursion into bull-goose crackpot conspiracy the likes of which hasn't been seen since Bill Cooper's magnum crapus, *Behold A Pale Horse*. In other words, it is the biggest crock to be foisted on the public in many moons - and as such, for those interested in what's going on in this weird conspiracy subculture, it is an absolute must read... Icke's main thesis in the book is that the world is being run by reptilian extraterrestrials who suck human blood, and that people like Hillary Clinton, Henry Kissinger, and the Queen of England are shape-changing reptiles from that ancient cold-blooded family line. His proof? None, except for the occasional wild rantings of the crayon-wielding crowd who attend his lectures and confess that they too ran into somebody who turned into a reptile in WalMart one time.' [8]

Before his new book was published I would have written of Icke that, like many of his American sources, his methodology is, roughly and unconsciously, if it is in print it must be true.[9] But in fact it is worse - or better - than this. In an e-mail from the Icke organisation about their on-line magazine, the following was given as the position of the organisation vis-à-vis truth, falsehood and so forth: 'Each article [in the Icke e-zine] is presented to give everyone every possible source to TRUTH available. *Discerning TRUTH is the responsibility of each reader*. We welcome challenging viewpoints from all sources... even opposing viewpoints. In diversity of views we can still find the research and documentation valuable, whether we agree with the views of the author or not.' (Emphasis added.)

In other words they are not interested in what is true and what is not;[10] or have given up trying to work out which is which. (Or simply do not care...) This almost postmodern disdain for what used to be called unselfconsciously 'objective reality' is, unfortunately, common among contemporary chroniclers of the conspiracy theory subculture of America. One of the best of the websites doing this, *The Konformist*, for example, regularly puts out conspiracy theories which the site's manager, Robert Sterling, who is no dummy, knows to be fatuous. There may be rationales for distributing junk knowledge but the basic reason is simple enough: most of the contemporary conspiracy theories would take months to check - if they were checkable at all. If the hosts of conspiracy-theory websites only posted what they knew or reasonably surmised to be true - or even plausible! - there would be little worth posting.

As the editor of this series, Paul Duncan, suggested to the author, among the audience for contemporary theories there does appear to be a section which simply does not care if the theories are true or not, who reads them simply as entertainment, perhaps in the same way that some people read Science Fiction and Fantasy. This would not matter were it not for the fact that this audience appears to encourage the indiscriminate generation and circulation of junk conspiracy theories; and these muddy the pond for those of us trying to peer through the silt to see what is going on down there at the bottom. Or is this merely the complaint of an out-of-date old empiricist still clinging to the delusion that it is possible to work out 'what really happened'?

cf. Dean !

Notes

1. There is an interesting fictional account of how the FOIA system works in Jim Hougan's 'novel of conspiracy,' *Kingdom Come* (New York: Ballantine, 2000).

2. See *The Independent*, 18 February 2000.

3. The most recent British example of which I have personal knowledge concerns a man, wrongfully convicted of murder who, now out of prison, is having his attempts to set up a small business disrupted by some branch of the state constantly blocking incoming telephone calls from potential customers. For the details of another such campaign see the account of the harassment of Armen Victorian in *Lobster* 29. Victorian's offence? He used the American Freedom of Information Act to request documents in areas the US military would rather were left alone.

4. An e-mail from Andy Winiarczyk at the Last Hurrah Bookshop in America, (tel. 570-321-1150) on Friday, 7 January 2000, gave details of 18 books (and one CD-ROM) on the JFK assassination I had not heard of, 6 published in the previous year. Kennedy buffs occasionally find themselves wondering if burying the researchers under mountains of paper isn't the objective of the declassification process...

5. Author of *Behold A Pale Horse*, which I have not read (life is too short), Cooper appeared at the Global Conspiracy Conference held in London in 1993. I saw a videotape of his presentation. Cooper claimed that Kennedy was shot by the driver of the car he was in. He showed an enormous - maybe 10 foot square - blow-up of one frame from the famous Zapruder film of the JFK assassination and asked the audience if they could see the driver shooting JFK. "No," said the audience. "That's because they've scraped the emulsion off the film," said Cooper. Duuuh... As happens occasionally, the paranoid is half-right. Cooper's belief that Zapruder's film has been doctored is correct - but not in the way he suggests. See the long and immensely complicated analysis in Mike Pincher, J D and Roy Schaeffer, 'The Case For Zapruder Film Tampering: The Blink Pattern' in *Assassination Science*, ed. James H Fetzer Ph.D. (Chicago: Catfeet Press, 1997; distributed in the UK by Eurospan). This micro example illustrates perfectly the difference between serious conspiracy research and conspiracy theories. The analysis of the blink pattern of the hazard lights of the presidential lim-

68

ousine car in the Zapruder film shows that the film has been edited. To find this out, to stand it up, and to write it out in sufficient detail to convince a reader, was difficult. All Cooper did was have a thought. At the bottom line: Cooper has no evidence that the emulsion had been scraped off the film...

6. The current belief of David Icke expressed in his 1999 book *The Biggest Secret: The Book That Will Change The World*, reviewed by Jim Keith in *The Konformist*, 22 June 1999.

7. This was later portrayed as comedy in the Mel Gibson, Robert Downey Jnr. film, *Air America*. The film was very loosely based on a section of the book *The Invisible Air Force* by Christopher Robbins (London: Pan, 1981).

8. www.konformist.com/1999/icke-keith.htm. When Keith died in late 1999 after going into hospital for a relatively minor operation, some of his colleagues wondered if his death really was an accident, titillating themselves with the idea that, hey, maybe they are a threat to someone.

9. In this performance Icke tells his audience that his interest in these areas began when, after a meeting in Hull, someone gave him a carrier bag full of cuttings. Since I live in Hull, let me state here that it was not me!

10. The second issue of the David Icke e-magazine is at www.david-icke.com/icke/magazine/vol-2/vol2.html.

6. Disinformation

The whole aim of practical politics is to keep the populace alarmed - and thus clamorous to be led to safety - by menacing it with an endless series of hobgoblins, all of them imaginary.

- H L Mencken

Intelligence agencies - the secret arms of the state - as well as being among the most important conspirators and sources of conspiracy in the modern world, have also been among the generators of conspiracy theories since World War 2. One of the skills acquired during the war was black propaganda; and with the onset of the Cold War both sides began churning out disinformation about their opponents, much of it delivered to contested areas in the developing world. For example, in the wake of the Kennedy assassination both the Soviet and French intelligence services put out conspiracy theories about the killing. The Soviets spread their disinformation blaming the CIA through an Italian newspaper and thence into a French-language Canadian paper, thence into the JFK researcher community, and eventually into the investigation of Jim Garrison (Kevin Costner in the movie *JFK*).[1] The core information in this theory turned up in another well-known document in the JFK conspiracy world, *The Torbitt Memorandum*. This also looks like disinformation to me - again probably Soviet in origin - although to date no one from the former Soviet bloc intelligence services has claimed the authorship of either. French intelligence personnel published a famous book in the JFK assassination world called *Farewell America*. Both blamed the CIA for the shooting.[2]

For example: employees of the US and Israeli governments, with assistance from some British personnel, invented and spread the conspiracy theory that the KGB, using the Bulgarians, shot the present Pope, John Paul, in 1981. A former CIA station chief no less, Paul Henze, wrote the first book articulating this nonsense;[3] and the theme was taken up enthusiastically by other CIA assets, including the late journalist Claire Sterling. In retaliation the Soviets invented and spread the conspiracy theory that AIDS was a biological weapon developed by the US army designed to kill people of colour.[4]

Occasionally such disinformation operations go horribly wrong. The KGB-shot-the-Pope allegation seems to have been part of a wider disinformation operation run by US intelligence people in the early 1980s to portray the Soviet Union as the world's major sponsor of terrorism. Some of this material was fed out to selected intelligence assets, one of them being the late Claire Sterling who wrote it up as the 1981 book *The Terror Network*.[5] At this juncture the US Secretary of State was Alexander Haig, who had made some bellicose speeches about the Soviets-as-sponsors-of-terror, then asked the CIA to provide him with the evidence. Alas the CIA's 'National Intelligence Estimate' on the subject of Soviet sponsorship of terrorism failed to support Haig's charges. Unfortunately, the Director of the CIA, William Casey, read the Sterling book and, unaware that the book was the result of a CIA disinformation project, began complaining to the authors of the CIA's report on Soviet sponsorship of terrorism that there was more information in this book than they had put in the Intelligence Estimate on the subject![6]

The British state had an organisation called the Information Research Department. It was set up originally in 1948, staffed with personnel from the wartime black propaganda organisations, with the stated aim of combating Soviet propaganda. But as soon as the politicians' backs were turned it reverted back to what its employees knew best - disinformation. It survived till 1977, employing hundreds of people, barely noticed by the politicians, putting out unattributable (i.e. anonymous) briefings, some true, some grey (i.e. half-true) and some black (i.e. false) through contacts in the print and broadcasting media made during the coldest parts of the Cold War. It turned up in all the post-World War 2 conflicts between the British colonial authorities and nationalist liberation movements in the British colonies, spreading the department 'line,' its conspiracy theory: the Commies are behind it all. And if there was no evidence that the Soviets were behind the troubles in, say, Cyprus, IRD would fabricate some.[7] In 1971 a senior member of the department was detached to Northern Ireland to work with the British Army there in the struggle with the IRA. He set up a psychological warfare unit called Information Policy which operated under cover of the press office in the British Army HQ in Lisburn. Information Policy began putting out material - a lot of it forged documents - claiming that the KGB was behind the Provisional IRA and

71

that the Labour Party was riddled with Communists or fellow-travellers and supported the IRA.[8]

The disinformation war within the Cold War has yet to be looked at in any detail, but my guess would be that we will eventually discover that quite substantial chunks of what we thought was history had been faked.

Disinformation About UFOs

The most recent area in which apparently official disinformation is now being generated is UFOs. In British UFO magazines in 1996/7 we had a stream of tales of secret bases in Britain, aliens, dead bodies all over the place, and secret army units running round the UK cleaning up the mess. Some of the accounts in these stories were not that far removed from a British version of Will Smith and Tommy Lee Jones in the *Men In Black* movie.[9] While claims of secret bases and secret units are a common feature of American UFO conspiracy theories, these stories were the first concerted attempt to get such themes established here. None of the stories were convincing. Secret bases are plausible in the United States because the deserts of the south western United States are so vast and so inaccessible it is easy to imagine the US military hiding all manner of facilities down there. But in the UK this kite simply will not fly because the country is so small. None of these British stories appear to have been checked by the magazines concerned before publication - how you would convincingly check allegations of secret Army units is unclear to me - and in all these stories the sources of information are anonymous; all claim to be serving or former military personnel; and, oddly enough, all have decided that the best forum for their extraordinary, earth-shattering story is not the *News Of The World*, let alone *Panorama* or the House of Commons, but a British UFO magazine. One researcher in the field I know was even rung up by someone claiming to be a London taxi driver, who proceeded to run the ancient old gag about the government official who had left a briefcase full of secret documents about the aliens and government in his cab. Given that my friend is ex-directory, he wondered how a London taxi driver had got his number. The documents were not forthcoming, of course; and all the contact did was inform my friend (a) that a disinformation exercise was underway, and (b) it was being run by incompetents.

We know there are official disinformation programmes being run in this field in the United States. The best analysed is that which climaxed with the 'leaking' of the so-called MJ12 documents purporting to detail a long-standing programme of secret research by US government officials into aliens and their spacecraft. Before the fabricated MJ12 documents were released, another researcher, Paul Bennewitz, and Linda Moulton Howe, who made the film *Strange Harvest*, about the cattle mutilation phenomenon, were shown similar documents.[10] Ms Howe told the journalist C B Bryan how she was invited to the Kirkland Air Force Base where, in the Air Force Office of Special Investigations, she met one of its staff who told her that her film had 'upset some people in Washington.' As a result, his superiors had asked him to brief her. She was shown a document called - wait for it - 'Briefing Paper For The President Of The United States On The Subject Of Identified Aerial Vehicles (IAVs) - IAVs.' This contained a history of US Government retrieval 'of crashed discs and alien bodies, dead and alive.' The notorious Roswell incident was just one of several. But Howe was not allowed to make notes or copies of this document, just to read it.[11]

This is precisely the disinformation technique used by Colin Wallace in the British Army's psychological operations unit in Belfast in the 1970s.[12] Wallace would take journalists, especially foreign journalists with a limited understanding of British politics, into a back room and show them 'secret documents' which they could read but not copy. Some of the documents were genuine, some forgeries. We have copies of some of the forgeries.[13] Alas, when Ms Howe was given the same treatment, no warning bell seems to have rung. Which is rather odd, for here was the US Air Force apparently deciding to let her in on the story they had spent so much time and money previously trying to deny or rubbish. She lapped all this up and has been recycling it, as per US Air Force psy-ops plan, ever since.

The purpose of the various disinformation operations in the UFO field of which we have glimpses is unclear. They may simply be rerunning the operations of the 1950s in which the CIA and other government agencies encouraged the belief in UFO sightings to provide 'cover' for their secret aircraft. (Seen a bright shining object high in the sky, Mildred? It is a UFO - not a US U-2 spy-plane on its way to photograph the Soviet Union at 65,000 feet.) This has been suggested as the explanation for the strange events at Area 51, the US Air Force's

73

testing base in the desert. Better to have the curious visitor think he or she has seen a collection of UFOs flying at night over the mountains which surround the base than believe the US is testing a variety of experimental planes about which Congress has not been informed.

It is certainly the case that the Area 51 story over the past 10 years or so bears all the hallmarks of a disinformation exercise: leaks, dribbles of information; one apparently authoritative witness, Jim Lazar who, upon closer scrutiny, starts to look less solid than he did at first.[14] This is a classic disinformation technique. The investigator is led off down the garden path and shown apparently good evidence to support the line of inquiry. Then his or her subject matter is exploded and the investigator is left with nothing. In the strange world of the psy-warriors this technique is known as the double-bubble.

It has been claimed that something like the 'double bubble' technique has been used in the United States against the media. Dr C B Scott Jones, one of the people most closely involved in the curious area where UFO researchers meet politicians and the military-intelligence complex, offered this as an explanation of the disinformation operations:

> 'Earlier I asked the question why there was no press response to Reagan's extraordinary statements concerning a space threat to the world. The short answer is that the press has effectively been taken out of the loop by the success of a counterintelligence programme targeted against the American public and the press. The government wants no restrictions on how it attempts to handle what we are calling UFO phenomena. To get this freedom of action, a clamp of secrecy and stealth intimidation of the press has been employed. The programme has been so successful against the press, that it doesn't even recognise the wound. The process apparently was to stage a number of 'UFO events,' get the press charging to the bait and then with fanfare show that it was either a hoax or misinterpretation of natural phenomena. When print editors hear: "UFO, UFO," we get the same response from them that the village finally gave the young sheep herder who cried "Wolf" too many times.' [15]

On the other hand there are obvious similarities between today's conspiracy theories portraying America threatened by extraterrestrial aliens, and the post-World War 1 and World War 2 scares that portrayed American threatened by human aliens. After World War 1 the 'aliens' were immigrants from Europe, some with socialist beliefs; after World War 2 they were a secret network of Communist agents.[16] It is striking that the recent explosion of stories about alien abductions and UFOs in America have coincided with the collapse of the Communist Threat. Among some sections of those studying the UFO phenomenon the suspicion is growing that some of these stories are disinformation being produced by the US military/intelligence bureaucracies, possibly to generate a new threat to replace the Red Menace and so allow the US military/intelligence bureaucracies to continue to consume 50% or so of total US tax revenues. To do that they have to have a plausible enemy; and since the Berlin Wall fell in 1989, such an enemy has not been available. With all due respect to Saddam Hussein, or the cocaine industry in Colombia, they are hardly a substitute for the Soviet empire and its ability to be portrayed as a worldwide and imminent threat to the USA.

Teaching Aliens To Line-Dance

How do we tell which conspiracy theories or allegations of conspiracy are worth taking seriously? There are no special rules. The plausibility of a conspiracy theory is determined in the same way that any other proposition - or theory - is: it is about reasons, rationality, weight of evidence. Just as in any other field, after a while you get a 'feel' or a 'nose' for what is and is not likely to be worth pursuing. In general, the smaller the event allegedly explained by a conspiracy, the more likely it is to be worth taking seriously. We know what kinds of real conspiracies are routinely exposed: a government agency out of control, a bureaucracy covering up something embarrassing, a witness threatened or murdered, the Masons influencing a local council - these sorts of things are not improbable. Much less probable are mega conspiracies. The world being as strange as it is, it is difficult to say for certain that anything is impossible. OK, the odds on David Icke's latest vision of the world run by shape-shifting reptiles turning out to be true look long, long, long. But other than something as bizarre as that, the

75

boundaries of the plausible have been pushed out a long way - not least by some of the mind-control technology discussed in the next section.

Take UFOs for example. It is now preposterous to deny the existence of UFOs: there are too many reliable witnesses, too many former government officials from both sides of the former Iron Curtain who have acknowledged government interest in the subject, too many bits of film and videotape from all over the world. But from there to the Alien Sex Fiend Abduction stories, or the alien-US elite alliance, is an enormous step. UFOs remain just that: *Unidentified* Flying Objects. That they exist cannot be rationally denied. But to go beyond that it gets pretty iffy pretty quickly. There is no reliable evidence that I am aware of for the existence of aliens: no artefacts, no photographs, no indisputable film or videotape. There is only human memory - notoriously unreliable human memory; and if you are willing to treat human memory as 'evidence' you end up dealing with what I now think of as the Betty Trout Problem.

Betty Trout is a State Director of the major American UFO organisation MUFON. At MUFON's 1999 symposium she described how, in one of her abduction episodes, she noticed that the 'hybrids' - beings allegedly part alien and part human - among whom she was, appeared to be wearing cowboy boots and hats. Betty Trout taught line-dancing classes and she realised she had been abducted that evening to teach 'hybrids' to line-dance.[17]

The Lammers accept the legitimacy of human memory. In their recent book MILABS, they discuss accounts of alien abduction but emphasise those in which 'abductees' describe meeting normal (American) military personnel, and sometimes 'aliens' working with normal military personnel, conducting the same range of quasi-medical procedures on the 'abductees' as reported elsewhere. Having made this selection of the 'data' they offer as hypotheses the following: 'It seems to us that there are indications that more than one human agenda, possibly three, may be involved in the currently unexplained alien abduction phenomenon... one group may be interested in advanced mind-and-behaviour-control experiments... a second group seems to be interested in biological or genetic research... a third group seems to be a military task force, which has been operating since the 1980s... '[18]

76

The Lammers' book is an interesting piece of speculation - but that is all it is. The Lammers chose to select 'abductees' who have 'seen' soldiers or human scientists. These 'abductees' are presumed to be reporting what they have 'seen' when they were, literally, abducted. But if these 'abductees' are reporting accurately, on what grounds do we determine that other 'abductees,' who do not report seeing soldiers or scientists, are not reporting accurately? Would the Lammers accept, for example, that Betty Trout was literally abducted and did, literally, meet hybrids, and did literally teach them to line-dance? And if they would not, which criteria would they use to distinguish between Betty Trout's story and the stories they do believe?

The Lammers suspect that the experience of 'alien abduction' is being synthetically generated by state personnel for reasons unknown. Their book opens with a quotation from the faintly mysterious and very spooky Dr C B Scott Jones. In 1994 Scott Jones had meetings with Dr John Gibbons, the scientific advisor to President Clinton, at which various bits of evidence about UFOs were presented to Gibbons. On February 17 1994 Scott Jones said to Gibbons, inter alia: "...I urge you to take another look in the *UFO Matrix of Belief* that I provided you last year. My mention of mind-control technology at the February 4 meeting was quite deliberate. Please be careful about this. *There are reasons to believe that some government group has interwoven research about this technology with alleged UFO phenomena.* If that is correct, you can expect to run into early resistance when inquiring about UFOs, not because of the UFO subject, but because that has been used to cloak research and applications of mind-control activity." (Emphasis added)[19]

Given Scott Jones' status and his years of access to high-level military, intelligence and political circles in the US, this comment of his is extremely interesting. But if he knows anything substantial about these mind-control experiments, to my knowledge he has chosen not to reveal it.

Mind Control

Once you make that initial move of not rejecting out of hand the more outlandish claims and try to deal with these areas rationally, it tends to get complicated in a hurry. Scott Jones referred to mind-control experiments, which is one of the subjects generating a great deal of conspiracy-theorising at the moment. We know that the US military, the CIA, and their Soviet counterparts, were busy in the 50s and 60s looking for a means of controlling the human mind. Drugs, hypnosis and electromagnetic fields were all investigated by scientists funded by the US (and Soviet) taxpayer.[20] But there are now hundreds of people, in Europe and in the USA - I know someone dealing with over 100 such cases in the USA - claiming to have been the victims of mind-control experiments. I have the written statements of half a dozen such putative victims in this country. Some claim to have electronic devices implanted in their head, or their body; some claim they are being bombarded by energy weapons of some kind, mostly microwaves.

The distribution of victims suggests that, just as in the 1950s and 60s and the MK-Ultra/MK-Delta programme and their predecessors,[21] the American military farmed out bits of the experiments to other members of NATO. Canada features in some of the early reports; as does Sweden. The best documented case in this country is that of the late Mr and Mrs Anthony Verney who died after being irradiated with extremely low frequency radiation.[22] I have seen X-rays which show implants in the brain of an individual in Sweden.[23] Brain scans are now available on home-pages on the Net, apparently showing the same sort of thing. There are now companies in the USA which, for a large amount of money, will debug your body. They will check you out - and remove, if necessary - bugs, implants, chips, whatever.

A Freedom of Information application by Jane Affleck produced a document from 1970, a report published by the Office of Technological Utilisation in NASA called *Implantable Biotelemetry Systems* - implants, in short. Thirty years ago they had them down to the size of a 5p coin. This 1970 report shows them, even gives wiring diagrams. Now some of them are practically invisible, like a strand of hair. Or so it is said.[24]

I have met two intelligent, educated people, who tell me they hear voices in their heads - the voices of teams of psychologists and intelligence personnel monkeying around with their brains. (This is sometimes called synthetic telepathy.) I have corresponded with others. The stories of other, intelligent, apparently otherwise normal people who claim to be receiving the voices are available on the Net. I could just say they are paranoid schizophrenics, one of the classic symptoms of which is hearing voices in your head. But I have known some schizophrenics and these two people do not seem like schizos to me (and neither do the others whose accounts I have merely read). And here's the problem: even if they did sound nutty it still would not be possible to dismiss them because the technology to do what they claim is being done to them exists. As far back as 1962 an American scientist called Alan Frey demonstrated that, using a microwave beam, you could transmit sounds - words - into the head of an individual that were inaudible to other people - 'voices in the head.'

There are people who have had implants put into their bodies; the evidence of this is now irrefutable. Microwave mind-control devices do exist - and if the testimony of the alleged victims is to be believed, some of these devices do work as claimed. The US Patent Office contains shoals of systems for influencing or manipulating minds registered in the last 20 years; and not in the Patent Office will be the systems the US state has decided are important to national security which we will never see. Before its collapse the Soviet Union was engaged in parallel research and there have been a series of reports in the last decade from what is now Russia suggesting that some of these devices have been deployed. Should we be surprised to learn that the CIA or some other branch of the US government (or its NATO allies) was doing random tests of this mind-control technology? That is what they did with various nerve agents and experimental drugs in the 50s - slipped them into people's drinks and just sprayed them round to see what happened. For the military scientists trying out their new weapons, their tests have the most perfect cover of all: no one will believe the victims babbling about voices in the head or invisible rays. Though the victims of this technology have been complaining since the late 1980s, it was only towards the end of last year that the first public demonstration took place in this country protesting against the use of this technology; and thus far the major media has declined to pay attention, preferring to dismiss the victims as crazies.[25]

I wonder at the state of R's evidence for some of this.

It is difficult to be optimistic about this situation changing quickly. These technologies are now among the most sensitive of military/intelligence secrets; and such secrets are difficult to expose. The CIA's early experiments in the field in the 1950s were kept secret until the late 1970s; the US government's various misuses of nuclear radiation in the United States in the early years of the Cold War were only addressed during Bill Clinton's first term; and the CIA's involvement in the drug trade, first described in the 1970s, is only now, reluctantly, being addressed. In this country, apparently afraid of a torrent of compensation claims, the government is still unwilling to acknowledge that the use of organophosphates in sheep dip has seriously injured hundreds of farmers. If dangerous chemicals in sheep dip is too awkward a subject for the British state to deal with, how much more reluctant will it be to acknowledge that some of its citizens have been the unwitting subjects of mind-control experiments? Sadly, the victims of the mind-control experiments of the last 20 years in the NATO countries are probably condemned to decades of marginalisation and ridicule.

Notes

1. This was first exposed by my erstwhile colleague, Stephen Dorril, in an essay in *Lobster* 2. This is now available on the web at http://mcadams.posc.mu.edu/lobster.htm.

2. I asked a retired SIS officer who his circle thought had done the deed when they first heard of it in 1963. "The CIA," he said. This was also apparently the belief of the Kennedy family.

3. *The Plot To Kill The Pope* (Beckenham, Kent: Croom Helm, 1984).

4. On the disinformation about the shooting of the Pope see Edward S Herman and Frank Brodhead, *The Rise And Fall Of The Bulgarian Connection* (New York: Sheridan Square Publications, 1986). To my knowledge no one in what is now Russia has admitted that the Soviets invented the AIDS-as-biological-weapon story but it has been convincingly traced back to Soviet intelligence. See, for example, Christopher Andrew and Oleg Gordievsky, *KGB: The Inside Story* (London: Hodder and Stoughton, 1990), pp.528-9 and *Counterpoint: A Monthly Report On Soviet Active Measures*, vol. 3 no. 6, November 1987. (*Counterpoint* was US-funded propaganda about Soviet propaganda. It was based in the UK but moved back to the US after being exposed by this writer in an issue of the now defunct *Digger* magazine.)

5. Sterling died in 1995. See the obituaries in *The Independent*, 26 June 1995 and *The Guardian*, 29 June. Sterling was certainly an intelligence asset, and possibly even a CIA officer. The best response to her *Terror Network* nonsense was Edward Herman's *The Real Terror Network* (Boston: South End Press, 1982) which showed, without a great deal of difficulty, that the major sponsor of terrorism in the post-World War 2 years has been the United States.

6. This is discussed in 'Anti-Diplomacy, Intelligence Theory And Surveillance Practice' by James Der Derian in *Espionage: Past, Present, Future* ed. Wesley K Wark (London: Frank Cass, 1994).

7. For an example from the Cyprus war see Charles Foley, *Legacy Of Strife: Cyprus From Rebellion To Civil War* (Harmondsworth: Penguin, 1964) p.104.

8. On this see Paul Foot, *Who Framed Colin Wallace?* (London: Macmillan, 1990). Some of the forgeries are reproduced in this volume.

9. See for example, '580 Security' in *Global UFO Investigation*, June/July 1997; 'UFO Crash In North Wales,' *UFO*, September/October 1996; the untitled essay in *Unopened Files* No 1, pp.5-19; 'Programmable Life Forms' in *Truth Seekers Review* 9. Thanks to Kevin McClure for bringing these to my attention.

10. On Bennewitz see Jim Marrs, *Alien Agenda* (London: Harper-Collins, 1997) pp.111-2. It is possible that the climax of this operation was the 'discovery' of the notorious film apparently showing an alien auto psy. This would make operational sense but there is, as yet, no evidence linking that piece of film to the documents. (And if the deception operation was any good, no such evidence will ever be found.)

11. C B Bryan, *Close Encounter Of The Fourth Kind*, (London: Weidenfeld and Nicolson, 1995). This is an account of the first big conference on the abduction phenomenon held at the Massachusetts Institute of Technology (MIT) and conveys vividly the complexity and oddity of the alien abduction story. On disinformation within the UFO world see also Armen Victorian, *Mind Controllers*, (London: Vision, 1999), pp.182-4.

12. And by IRD in Cyprus. See the reference in note 7 above.

13. Some of these are reproduced in Paul Foot's *Who Framed Colin Wallace?*

14. Go to www.serve.com/mahood/lazar/lazarmn.htm for a long, detailed, sceptical analysis of Lazar.

15. From Dr C B Scott Jones, 'UFOs And New Frontiers: Connecting With The Larger Reality.' This was e-mailed to me and I don't know where it was first published.

16. Such a network did exist, though how threatening it was is debatable. See Allan Weinstein and Alexander Vassiliev, *The Haunted Wood: Soviet Espionage In America - The Stalin Era* (New York: Random House, 1999) and John Early Haynes and Harvey Klehr, *Venona: Decoding Soviet Espionage In America* (New Haven (USA) and London: Yale University Press, 1999).

17. The Betty Trout story was reported in Kevin McClure's newsletter *Abduction Watch*, July 1999. If 'Betty Trout' sounds familiar you may be remembering the character Kilgore Trout from Kurt Vonnegut's novel *Breakfast Of Champions*. Kilgore Trout was also the author of the spoof sf novel *Venus On The Half-Shell* (London: W H Allen, 1976, Grenada/Panther, 1982)

18. Dr Helmut Lammer and Marion Lammer, *MILABS: Military Mind Control And Alien Abduction* (Lilburn, GA (USA): Illuminet Press, 1999) p.29.

19. On Scott Jones see Armen Victorian, *Mind Controllers* (London: Vision, 1999) pp.180-2.

20. The basic text on the American end of this remains John Marks, *The Search For The Manchurian Candidate* (London: Allan Lane/Penguin Books, 1979). For an introduction to this issue written from an American legal point of view, 'The Law And Mind Control,' go to http://members.aol.com/smartnews/fivecases.htm.

21. In the 1950s the CIA embarked on a large number of programmes investigating the effects of drugs, hypnosis, magnetism and various electrical devices, on the brain. The programmes were codenamed MK-Ultra, MK-Delta, MK-Naomi and so on. The programmes have never been fully documented because the files were destroyed in the 1970s when the US Congress began sniffing around them. Fragments of the CIA's documentation of the programmes were found in accounting files and from these fragments some of the programmes have been partially reconstructed. On this see John Marks in note 20 above.

22. See Armen Victorian, *Mind Controllers* (New York/London: Vision/North Atlantic Books, 1999), chapters 7 and 8.

23. See Mind Control Forum www.mk.net/~mcf/ which opens with pictures of the Swede, Robert Naeslund, and the implants in his head. Given Sweden's unpleasant track record in eugenics, it seems an appropriate place to find people having involuntary implants put in their brains. www.webcom.com/~pinknoiz/coldwar/microwave.html contains a pretty reasonable picture of how this subject looked to intelligent Americans three or four years ago.

24. For a survey of some recent US patents in this field see Armen Victorian, 'The Military Use Of Electromagnetic Microwave And Mind Control Weapons' in *Lobster* 34 which is reprinted in *Mind Controllers* (see note 19 above).

25. The demo was the work of the Project Freedom Network, campaigning against what it calls 'remote mind-control weapons.' According to a letter from Mr Farquhar, the Project's leader, on 19 October 1999 they held a demonstration outside the House of Commons attended by 'around 15 supporters' 'about half' of whom 'claim to be the victims of psychotronic attacks.' Mr Farquhar chained himself to the railings in the hope of being arrested but the police declined to do the honours. Project Freedom is forming a Psychotronic Attack victim support group, details of which - along with photographs of the demonstration - can be found on their website www.isleofavalon.co.uk/local/h-pages/pro-freedom/.

7. Conspiracy Theories And Conspiracies

The role of elite management groups such as the Trilateral Commission and Bilderberg Group is one of the strands in the wonderful, wacky, world of contemporary conspiracy theory worth taking seriously; and it is now almost exclusively the territory of the radical right. This was not always the case. When Jimmy Carter, hitherto an obscure southern governor, appeared as a front runner in the race for the 1976 US presidency, sections of the American left became interested in the role of the Trilateral Commission of which he had been a member. This brief flurry of interest led to the 1980 book *Trilateralism*, still the best single volume on the elite management group.[1] Bill Clinton was also another obscure southern governor until being adopted by the Trilateral Commission. Is this a coincidence? No, it is not. For the Democratic Party has a recurring problem when it comes to finding a plausible presidential candidate: the coalition of groups which elects a Democrat president includes the so-called Dixiecrats, white Democrats in the southern states. To get their votes and the votes of the black Americans of the northern cities is a neat trick: hence the recurring appeal of televisual, southern Democratic governors - good old boys - to the corporate leaders of America thinking of the presidency. One of the roles of the Trilateral Commission in the United States - like the Bilderberg Group in Europe - is to assess politicians and promote those deemed acceptable by the corporate managers.

There is another conspiracy strand or tradition and in a very general sense this is the territory of the Anglo-American left. Loosely, this distinction could be put like this. The right is interested in conspiracies it perceives are undermining some kind of natural or desired order, plotting against the will of the people, the constitution, the national interest, etc. - what we might call conspiracies *against* the state. The Communist conspiracy theory, the Jewish banker theory and the current crop of New World Order, one world, elite dominance theories are examples of this. The liberal left, on the other hand, is chiefly interested in conspiracies committed *by* the state. From where I am on the left side of the fence, quite why these two areas are so distinct is unclear to me: an interest in the elite management groups (right) should fit comfortably with an interest in the big scandals - say Iran-Contra (left). In practice, however, the right's desire to preserve - or conserve -

the existing order, no matter how critical they also may be of it, gener-ally precludes them acknowledging the crimes and conspiracies of that order; and the left is unwilling to engage with a subject matter which has been 'contaminated' by interest from the right. And vice versa. This was vividly illustrated recently by the almost complete lack of interest shown by the American left in the massacre of the Branch Davidians at Waco, Texas, by federal forces.[2] Equally, that section of the American right which is so preoccupied with the elite management groups and the threat posed to their conception of America by the so-called New World Order, has shown no interest in the assassinations of the Kennedys and King, Watergate, Iran-Contra, etc., except to rubbish those trying to uncover the truth.

The liberal left strand of interest in conspiracies by the state begins with the Kennedy assassination in 1963 and the killings of Robert Kennedy and Martin Luther King in 1968; and from there runs seam-lessly through the Vietnam War, into Watergate and thence into all the related revelations of CIA and FBI operations which followed Water-gate.[3] If you started now and devoted yourself full-time to getting up to speed on the literature on the JFK killing alone it would take a year, maybe more. Let us go back, briefly, to 1963 and see if we can get a sense of why these assassinations of almost 40 years ago are not only relevant but seminal.

In 1963 there was virtually no investigative journalism; large chunks of the US mass media had been co-opted by the CIA in the pro-paganda war with the Soviet Union.[4] There was little autonomous American left and much of what there was, we now know, was wholly or partly being run by the FBI.[5] The conspiracy theory writer, Robert Anton Wilson, recently described his own experiences of this: 'In the 1960s in Chicago, I was involved in the anti-war movement. Congres-sional investigators later revealed that there were over 5000 govern-ment agents assigned to infiltrate peace groups in Chicago alone working for the Federal Bureau of Investigation (FBI), some for the Central Intelligence Agency (CIA) and some for Army Intelligence. From 1968 on, the FBI was following a programme code-named COINTELPRO. The purpose of COINTELPRO was to make sure the anti-war movement knew it was infiltrated, in order to spread suspi-cion, distrust and paranoia among individuals and groups who might otherwise have co-operated harmoniously. Working in the peace movement in those days was, accordingly, like living in an Eric Ambler novel. In any given week I would be warned perhaps three times that somebody I trusted was really a government agent and, of course, somebody who was accused one day might very well be around to accuse somebody else the next day. Over 20 years later, I still don't know who was a government agent and who was not.' [6]

There was, in fact, little critical community of any kind in the USA in 1963. Those who went through the motions of sitting on the Warren Commission investigating the Kennedy assassination assumed that they would produce a report which no one would read and the whole thing would then be put to bed. Since the whole thing was, if not a charade then a less-than-serious attempt to get at the truth, the evidence haphazardly accumulated by the Commission's team of lawyers was thrown together higgledy-piggledy in the Warren Commission's famous 26 volumes of evidence, with no sense, no organisation and no index worth speaking of. It just never occurred to those in charge that anyone would bother to look. One of the Commission members, former CIA chief Allen Dulles, famously said of the *Report* that it would only be read by a few professors. He was wrong. A number of ordinary US citizens who felt the official version of the assassination was dodgy, to say the least, bought one of the 1000 copies of the evidence which the government had printed and then began poring over it. One woman indexed the 26 volumes. Almost immediately the shoddy nature of the investigation was revealed.

The Warren Commission and its team of lawyers were not tasked to investigate the shooting of JFK but to provide the evidence that Oswald, the 'lone nut,' had done it. We now know that one of the chief preoccupations of those in charge in the White House at the time was preventing the assassination being used by anti-Communist pressure groups within the US - the anti-Castro Cubans, notably - to trigger another invasion of Cuba by US forces. Within 24 hours of the shooting, the Attorney General, Nicholas Katzenbach, had decided that the whole thing better be shut down. In the collective Washington memory, the Cuban Missile Crisis of 1962 still loomed large. In that climate, who really shot Kennedy was never an issue. As far as we can judge from the memoirs of those around at the time, nobody seems to have cared greatly. The identity of Kennedy's killer was of little consequence when measured against the danger of another nuclear show-down with the Soviet Union.

The federal government's major investigative body, the FBI, was happy that there was to be no serious investigation because they were in danger of being exposed as grossly incompetent. If it was shown that Oswald, qua Communist, had done the deed for political reasons, they had failed to prevent a Communist shooting the president. And Oswald had been a very public Communist. He had been on TV as a Communist, was corresponding with the Communist Party of the USA, the American Socialist Workers Party, and the Fair Play for Cuba Committee - all of which were penetrated by the FBI. He had also defected to the Soviet Union and redefected; he was known to the FBI office in Dallas. In the Cold War years in the United States, in the southern United States, Lee Harvey Oswald was about as public a Communist as you could imagine. For the FBI to be exposed as not having prevented him, of all people, from shooting the president would have been a bureaucratic disaster. And there was the danger that Oswald would be revealed as an FBI informant, for which there is some evidence. So the 'lone nut' verdict suited the politicians, who did not want trouble with the Soviet Union; it suited the FBI; and it suited the other American agencies, including the CIA, with whom Oswald had been involved in his curious career.

In the big assassinations of the 1960s, the Kennedys and King, the conspiracy hinged on presenting the forces of law and order with a ready-made solution. Oswald was framed, but framed so crudely it is pretty obvious he was meant to be a dead assassin. What they had against him would never have stood up in court; and had he appeared in court he would have talked of his various intelligence roles.

In the killing of Martin Luther King the police were again involved. The patsy, James Earl Ray, was run round America, told to buy a rifle, and finally installed in a boarding house near the site of the shooting. The local police detailed to guard King were pulled off and King was shot. The rest was easy because the local police found a rifle and other bits and pieces with James Earl Ray's name on them, conveniently left near the scene of the crime. Voilà! case closed: everybody in Memphis law enforcement was happy; everybody, that is, except a black cop guarding King, who had been called away just before the shooting. James Earl Ray, threatened with the death penalty if he was tried and convicted, accepted a plea bargain, and confessed to something he hadn't done. So there was no trial: the evidence against Ray was not tested. Again, as with the JFK murder, there was no serious investigation by the authorities.[7]

With the Robert Kennedy murder it was more sophisticated - the patsy assassin did actually shoot at Kennedy in front of dozens of witnesses. Yet the American political and judicial system's refusal to take on board the RFK assassination is even more perverse than in the case of his brother. The autopsy evidence is absolutely clear that Robert Kennedy was shot at point-blank range behind his ear: his skin had power burns indicating a firing distance of no more than a couple of inches. But Sirhan, all eyewitnesses agree, was in front of him and never got close enough to inflict that wound. The obvious other candidate is a man called Thane Cesar who was working as a temporary security guard and was standing right behind Kennedy when he was shot. Robert Kennedy whirled round and tried to grab Cesar when he was shot. Some of the pictures of Kennedy dying on the floor in the hotel kitchen, show Cesar's bow tie on the floor next to him: Kennedy ripped it off. Cesar denies he did it and passed a lie-detector test on the question - if that means anything.[8]

The official verdicts remain that Oswald, Ray and Sirhan did the deeds, though the 1977 House Select Committee on Assassinations hedged their bets a little and concluded that John Kennedy was probably killed by a conspiracy. Having spent at least a decade in bed with the CIA, the major American media needed little persuading to accept the US government's 'lone assassin' verdict in JFK's case; and the other two seemed clear-cut: Ray confessed and Sirhan was seen firing at RFK.

All three assassinations hinged on local police forces either co-operating with the murders or not doing their jobs properly. All three relied on the major media and the political system not to ask questions. It is one of the striking political facts of post-World War 2 American history that the Democratic Party lost its two most charismatic figures and never generated much of a head of steam for a decent inquiry. Had it not been for the handful of sceptics back in the 60s poring over the Warren Commission evidence, the whole thing would have slipped into history just as Allen Dulles predicted.

The group of JFK assassination researchers in the 1960s chipped away at the Warren Commission, dismantling the report section by section. More importantly, in so doing they embarked on a long process of self-education about the nature of US politics and post-World War 2 history; and this, in turn, brought to the public's attention the role of agencies like the CIA which had hitherto been largely secret. By the time what became known as Watergate began to break in 1973, the majority of the American electorate had ceased to believe the Warren Commission and many were prepared to believe that the American government was capable of almost anything. (Thousands of dead American soldiers returning from Vietnam helped.)

The Kennedy assassination was the lens through which I, along with many other people, first began to study American politics. For the Kennedy assassination said: here is a society and a political system in which the president is shot in broad daylight and the body politic - his professional colleagues - did not feel able to look for the truth. No doubt part of that reluctance was engendered by the ideological and military competition with the Soviet Union (what did it say about the world's greatest democracy, the land of the brave, etc., that JFK got his head blown off on the street?) And no doubt the significance of this factor in the minds of those in Washington who created the 'lone assassin' myth was underestimated at the time by the first wave of JFK researchers. However the central point remains: 22 November 1963 was the moment when the collective post-World War 2 innocence of the American Dream ended and conspiracy research began.[9] And that is why, despite the fact that we are approaching the 40th anniversary of the event, the shots of 22 November 1963 are still ringing in the ears of American history.

Conspiracies are real and by no means necessarily the product of a paranoid imagination. If this essay has a single message, this is it. But as the Kennedy assassination showed, there is not just one big over-arching conspiracy; there are many smaller conspiracies - some of them competing, interlocking, overlapping. Lee Harvey Oswald had documented connections to the FBI and the CIA and his activities have led to serious research into whole areas of covert operations by both agencies about which the US public and political system was almost entirely ignorant in 1963: for example, the FBI's COINTELPRO operations against the American left. Oswald's one-man branch of the Fair

Play for Cuba Committee in New Orleans is obviously and certainly - but not yet provably - a part of the COINTELPRO operations against the national pro-Castro Fair Play for Cuba Committee. Jack Ruby was an FBI informant in the early 1950s and was the pay-off man between organised crime and the Dallas Police. Had there been a half-serious investigation of Kennedy's shooting in 1963/4, Oswald and Ruby alone would have led into the CIA's then still officially secret war against Cuba run out of Miami, the anti-Castro alliance formed between the CIA and the Mafia, not to mention the FBI's COINTEL-PRO operations. When Ruby shot Oswald all these organisations had reasons to cover up the truth about their connections to them. There was a conspiracy to murder Kennedy but there were many conspiracies after his death to suppress the truth and mislead the investigations which had nothing to do with the initial assassination conspiracy. It took many years for the JFK assassination research buffs to see past the idea that by researching the cover-up they would follow the trail back to the conspirators. There were too many cover-ups and too many trails. The cui bono? (who benefits?) question told us nothing in the Oswald murder case: everybody benefited from Oswald's death.

Near the beginning of this chapter I tried to draw a distinction between conspiracy theories on the right and conspiracy research on the left. I suggested - loosely - that the liberal left was interested in conspiracies by the state and that the conservative right was interested in conspiracies against the state. The distinction is still meaningful but the categories are less neat and tidy than they seemed in, say, 1975. There are people out there now who are neither right nor left but who are - or appear to be - simply conspiracy theorists. For example, is the research into the Oklahoma bombing - an alleged state conspiracy - coming from the right or the left? It appears to be coming from that section of the American right which believes that the overweening power of the federal authorities is the real culprit. (It is worth remembering that the culprit/patsy, Timothy McVeigh, was a supporter of the militias.) But where on the political spectrum is Ian Goddard, for example, who has been pushing hardest to get a decent investigation of the shooting-down of the plane TWA 800 off New York? Is he on the right or the left?[10] I do not know; and, more interestingly, I cannot tell from reading his work. Take another example, *Steamshovel*, which began somewhere on the anarchist left as a magazine then set up a website, in January announced its new, improved website, with the slogan 'all conspiracy, no theory.' And where would you place Jonathan Vanakin, author of *Conspiracies, Cover-Ups And Crimes* (New York: Dell, 1992), perhaps the best single volume guide to this field?

There is talk of a left-right fusion in this field, of an ideologically neutral conspiracy theory mindset - of a conspiracy-theory culture. This strikes me as implausible. While there may be subjects which both left and right might find of relevance - the obvious example being the role of the elite management groups like the Bilderbergers or Trilateralists - in the end, given the enormous amount of possible material, individual choice of subject will entail some kind of ideological orientation. In so far as there is anything resembling a conspiracy-theory culture or mindset, it is essentially an anarchist or libertarian viewpoint which says that since all states are corrupt, all states will contain - or will be - conspiracies against their citizens.

Political conspiracy is so routine, as a concept 'conspiracy' would be of little interest were it not for the refusal of our chattering classes to acknowledge its legitimacy. On the other hand, the political usefulness of 'conspiracy theorist' and 'conspiracy theory' to our ruling elite should not to be underestimated. That people interested in what the elite is doing can be dismissed as anoraks, conspiracy theorists and - the British journalists' favourite - 'people with an agenda,' is very useful to our rulers.[11] The process of being thus marginalised is described by Robert Parry. Working as a journalist for Associated Press in the 1980s, he began uncovering what became known as Iran-Contra and was rubbished by colleagues and political opponents in the Reagan administration as a 'conspiracy theorist.' [12]

The importance of conspiracies, not conspiracy theories, is political. The conspiracies we should be looking at most closely are those run by the state - in this benighted, secretive, country we might say the conspiracies which are the state - or by the supranational bodies such as the European Union and the transnational corporations and their fronts. The UFO-alien-conspiracy-abduction frenzy is perhaps the most fascinating puzzle this essay has surveyed; but the British-American Project contains four members of the current British Cabinet.[13] Despite the campaigns generated by the revelations of Peter Wright, Colin Wallace and Cathy Massiter in the late 1980s, the secret organisations of the British state remain unchallenged, unaccountable to the politicians and the electorate, their budgets still intact. I strongly suspect that the powers-that-be would be very happy if people like me concentrated on alien abductions rather than the parapolitical connections of the Blair faction in the Labour Party. (The mega conspiracy baloney - from Jewish bankers to shape-shifting reptiles in the White House - is simply background noise, a distraction; and it has sometimes occurred to me to wonder if some of it isn't being generated by state agencies precisely to distract us.)

Notes

1. Edited by Holly Sklar, this was subtitled *The Trilateral Commission And Elite Planning For World Management*, and published by South End Press in Boston in 1980. This is still in print but, though written from a left perspective, these days it is bought almost exclusively by those on the right.

2. Thus American columnist Alexander Cockburn: 'To this day one can meet progressive types who devote many of their waking hours to activities designed to save Mumia abu Jamal who didn't give a toss about the Branch Davidians and their terrible slaughter by the federal government, and who still don't. Use the word 'cult' and both reason and moral judgement enter recess.' From 'Waco And The Press' in *CounterPunch*, (USA) 8 September 1999.

3. The best JFK websites are *Deep Politics* www.njmetronet.com/jfkdpq and *Probe* www.webcom.com/ctka/Default.htm - but these are sites run for and by experts and specialists and would be virtually unintelligible to a beginner. The best, most comprehensive, single volume on the Kennedy assassination remains Anthony Summers' *The Kennedy Conspiracy*, the latest edition of which is from Warner Books, London, 1998. This is the place to start.

4. I do not know of any book-length study of this but see Carl Bernstein, 'The CIA And The Media' in *Rolling Stone* 20 October 1977.

5. See *COINTELPRO: The FBI's Secret War On Political Freedom* ed. Cathy Perkus (New York: Monad Press, 1975). More generally on the FBI's role in attacking the American left see Athan Theoharis and John Cox, *The Boss: J Edgar Hoover And The Great American Inquisition* (London: Harrap, 1989). The website www.crunch.com/01 lists thousands of declassified FBI files.

6. From Wilson's introduction to Donald Holmes, *The Illuminati Conspiracy - The Sapien System*, (New Falcon Publication, 655 East Thunderbird, Phoenix, AZ 85022, USA).

7. See William F Pepper, *Orders To Kill: The Truth Behind The Murder Of Martin Luther King*, (New York: Carroll and Graf, 1995). In December 1999 Pepper and the King family finally got to put their case for a conspiracy to the test in a civil suit. The jury found that King was murdered by a conspiracy. The AP report of the story is at www.washingtonpost.com/wp-srv/aponline/19991208/aponline182559_000.htm

8. On the RFK assassination and the role of Cesar see Dan Moldea, *The Killing Of Robert F Kennedy*, (London: W W Norton, 1995). After making an unanswerable case for a conspiracy in the first four-fifths of the book, in the final section Moldea tracks down Cesar and concludes, solely on the basis of a polygraph test, that Cesar is innocent and all the eyewitnesses and forensic evidence should be ignored.

9. This is not to suggest that pre-1963 there were no radical critics, no left, no investigative journalism - I F Stone, for one, comes to mind - just not very many.

10. Ian Williams Goddard, www.erols.com/igoddard; TWA-800 case core is at www.erols.com/igoddard/twa-core.htm.

11. 'Anorak' and 'trainspotter' are concepts used and popularised in recent years by journalists to denigrate people with longer attention spans than their own. Most journalists' idea of research is nipping down to the cuttings library and having a quick squint, making a couple of phone calls to someone half a step ahead of themselves, or phoning some press officer for the departmental line. Most of them work on stories for hours rather than days; let alone weeks or years. A part of them knows this is not good enough and they fend off this uncomfortable thought by dismissing those with deeper or longer interests as 'anoraks,' 'obsessives,' 'hobbyists,' and, the really useful one, 'people with an agenda.' Journalists are intensely suspicious of people with agendas - even if, perhaps especially if, that agenda is a desire to get at the truth about something.

12. See chapter 1, note 22.

13. Discussed in chapter 4.

The Essential Library

Why not try other titles in the Pocket Essentials library? Each is £2.99 unless otherwise stated. Look out for new titles every month.

New This Month @ £3.99 each:

Conspiracy Theories by Robin Ramsay
Marilyn Monroe by Paul Donnelley

Also Available

Film: **Woody Allen** by Martin Fitzgerald
Jane Campion by Ellen Cheshire
Jackie Chan by Michelle Le Blanc & Colin Odell
Joel & Ethan Coen by John Ashbrook & Ellen Cheshire
David Cronenberg by John Costello (£3.99)
Film Noir by Paul Duncan
Terry Gilliam by John Ashbrook
Heroic Bloodshed edited by Martin Fitzgerald
Alfred Hitchcock by Paul Duncan
Krzysztof Kieslowski by Monika Maurer
Stanley Kubrick by Paul Duncan
David Lynch by Michelle Le Blanc & Colin Odell
Steve McQueen by Richard Luck
Brian De Palma by John Ashbrook
Sam Peckinpah by Richard Luck
Slasher Movies by Mark Whitehead (£3.99)
Vampire Films by Michelle Le Blanc & Colin Odell
Orson Welles by Martin Fitzgerald

TV: **Doctor Who** by Mark Campbell

Books: **Cyberpunk** by Andrew M Butler (£3.99)
Philip K Dick by Andrew M Butler (£3.99)
Noir Fiction by Paul Duncan

Available at all good bookstores, or send a cheque to: **Pocket Essentials (Dept CT), 18 Coleswood Rd, Harpenden, Herts, AL5 1EQ, UK**. Please make cheques payable to 'Oldcastle Books.' Add 50p postage & packing for each book in the UK and £1 elsewhere.

US customers can send $5.95 plus $1.95 postage & packing for each book to: **Trafalgar Square Publishing, PO Box 257, Howe Hill Road, North Pomfret, Vermont 05053, USA**. tel: 802-457-1911, fax: 802-457-1913, e-mail: tsquare@sover.net

Customers worldwide can order online at **www.pocketessentials.com**, **www.amazon.com** and at all good online bookstores.